Village W
in
LINCOLNSHIRE

Brett Collier

COUNTRYSIDE BOOKS
NEWBURY BERKSHIRE

First published 1998

COUNTRYSIDE BOOKS
3 Catherine Road
Newbury, Berkshire

ISBN 1 85306 498 X

Designed by Graham Whiteman
Maps and photographs by the author
Illustrations by Trevor Yorke

Front cover photograph of Tealby taken
by Rod Edwards

Produced through MRM Associates Ltd., Reading
Typeset by Techniset Typesetters, Newton-le-Willows
Printed by J. W. Arrowsmith Ltd., Bristol

Contents

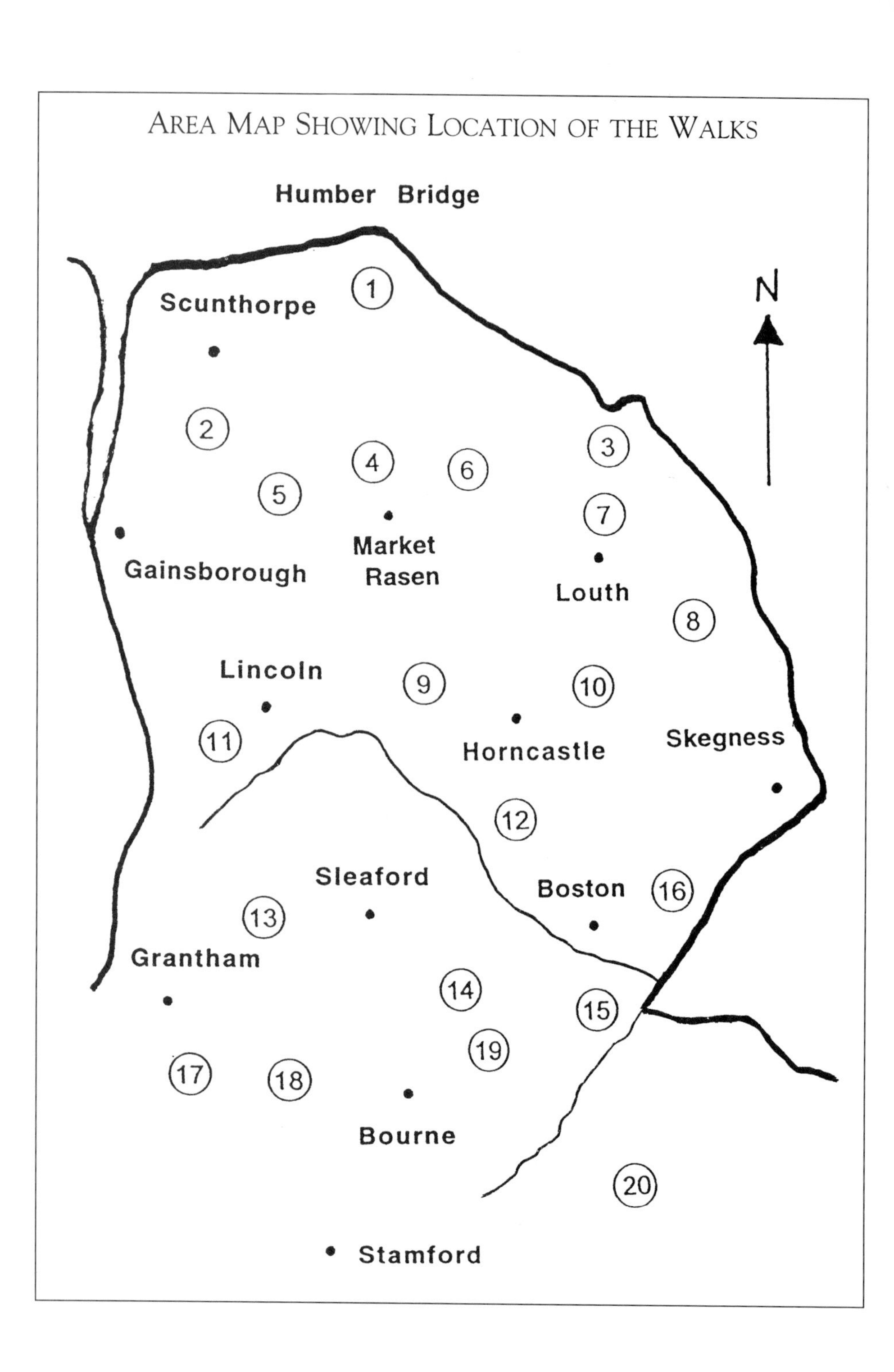

AREA MAP SHOWING LOCATION OF THE WALKS
Humber Bridge
N
Scunthorpe
1
2
5
4
6
3
7
Gainsborough
Market
Rasen
Louth
8
Lincoln
9
10
11
Horncastle
Skegness
12
Sleaford
Boston
16
13
Grantham
14
15
19
17
18
Bourne
20
Stamford

To Janet
who held the fort.

Publisher's Note

We hope that you obtain considerable enjoyment from this book; great care has been taken in its preparation. Although at the time of publication all routes followed public rights of way or permitted paths, diversion orders can be made and permissions withdrawn.

We cannot of course be held responsible for such diversion orders and any inaccuracies in the text which result from these or any other changes to the routes, nor any damage which might result from walkers trespassing on private property. We are anxious though that all details covering the walks are kept up to date and would therefore welcome information from readers which would be relevant to future editions.

Introduction

The book covers the sparsely populated 'old Lincolnshire' from the Humber to the Wash. The pace of life is slow here and there are miles and miles of empty fieldpaths waiting to be explored, with lots of space under wide horizons, be it farmland, heathland, wold, fen or saltmarsh. Lincolnshire, it has been said, is a flat county, full of unending cabbage fields and oil-seed rape and devoid of wildlife. It is not true, for Lincolnshire has some very important habitats, including some of the most important lime woods in Britain, and it is certainly not all flat.

One cannot really state which part of Lincolnshire is best for walking although many would opt for the Wolds. However, the Lincoln Edge, the Wolds, the Fens, Marshland and the Heath each have their own special attractions. The remote Gedney Hill with its spot height of three metres above sea level, Surfleet Seas End, many miles from the sea today, or Woolsthorpe by Colsterworth (there are two Woolsthorpes, not far apart) with its manor house and a descendant of a famous apple tree are all villages whose descriptions are to be found in the book. And lonely Sempringham, where a Welsh princess was held prisoner in the priory for all her life, Willoughby, one of whose sons became Admiral of New England and whose life was saved by an Indian princess, Pocahontas, and Goxhill, whose Haven is the most northerly point of the county, are all there to be explored. These are just a few of the places you are invited to visit, so make some 'quality time' to get out of the car and find areas of quite unexpected interest and beauty. There are some 90 miles between Goxhill and Gedney Hill which gives you plenty of scope.

Many of these villages, sometimes less than a mile off a familiar main road and whose names you have sighted on roadsigns for years, may be ones you have never contemplated visiting for there wasn't any reason to do so. Fotherby and Willoughton are two that well repay driving half a mile down the lanes to investigate. Village churchyards also often reveal quite unexpected interest, such as the auctioneer's gravestone at Corby Glen. This book, then, offers you an opportunity to change your routine, to investigate hitherto unexplored areas of the county and often, I'm quite sure, to be pleasantly surprised by what you discover.

The walks are all circular and vary in distance from 1½ to 6¾ miles. They are illustrated by sketch maps, designed to guide you to the starting point and give a simple but accurate idea of the route to be taken. However, the use of an Ordnance Survey map will greatly add to your enjoyment and understanding of an area, being particularly helpful for identifying the main features of views. Details of the relevant Landranger (1:50 000) sheets are therefore given.

The routes described are on public rights of way or, in a very few cases, permissive paths and all have been discussed with the appropriate authorities. Always attempt to follow the correct line of any public right of way for to seek alternative routes only confuses other walkers and may make you liable to a challenge from the landowner that you are nowhere near a public path. It is now an offence for any public right of way not to be clearly defined to its minimum width throughout all seasons of the year. However, Countryside Officers cannot be everywhere and it would be most helpful to report fieldpath obstructions of any kind to the Group Leader — Countryside, Environmental Services Directorate, Lincolnshire County Council, Newland, Lincoln LN1 1YL.

One of the most frequent complaints from members of the farming fraternity is that walkers leave litter, some of which may be harmful to livestock. It is a good idea therefore to leave the countryside better than you found it by collecting an item of litter en route. This is a positive response to the litter problem, it will make you feel virtuous and such action helps to demolish the argument regarding visitors and litter.

Places where food and drink can be obtained are given for each walk, except one where a picnic is suggested. Pub opening times have not been included because they often change and, in some cases, depend upon the seasons. However, details can always be obtained by using the telephone number which is given with each description and it is often wise to do so, particularly should you want a meal.

This brings us to the motor car. The lifeblood of any village is its inhabitants, and Lincolnshire has an abundance of villagers who really care for their environment. Therefore, please use the utmost discretion when parking vehicles. Car parking locations are indicated in the text — but if they are full, or for some reason unusable, do ensure that you park your vehicle in such a way as not to be a nuisance to those who live close by. Where the walks commence from the village inn, it must be stressed that parking is for patrons only. If you are leaving your car at a pub car park, especially out of normal opening times, it is courteous and friendly to leave a note that you are doing the walk and that you anticipate using the facilities of the hostelry upon your return. All the publicans know about the book and are looking forward to meeting new visitors to their establishments. This sort of courtesy generates much goodwill, for these days an unknown car left unattended for some time may provoke unnecessary suspicion. Not leaving your car by the favourite spot near the main entrance also helps!

Finally, we hope that you will enjoy this series of walks, and that you may be further encouraged to explore and get to know more of Lincolnshire's varied countryside.

John Clare (1793–1864) once wrote:

Oh take me from the busy road
I cannot bear the noise
For Nature's voice is never loud
I seek for quiet joys.

What John Clare would have thought about modern traffic today I shudder to think, but many of the places and walks in this book will, I hope, still offer 'quiet joys'.

Brett Collier

WALK 1

GOXHILL

Length : 3 miles

Getting there: From the A1077 Immingham to Barton upon Humber road turn off at Thornton Curtis, leading straight to Goxhill after 2½ miles.

Parking: There is usually space for parking at the end of King Street by All Saints church, or alternatively you could use the car park at the Brocklesby Hunt, if visiting the pub.

Maps: OS Landranger 112 Scunthorpe and 113 Grimsby — each map shows part of the walk (GR 103213).

A quiet, unassuming settlement well off the beaten track but one of Lincolnshire's loveliest villages with its combination of brick and pantile, old and new. Local people have a right to feel proud of their village with its delightful tree-lined streets, particularly the lovely avenue of cherry trees as one approaches in spring.

Hundreds of former United States Air Force men have evocative memories of Goxhill, renamed Goat Hill by servicemen, for it was their first base in wartime England. During World War II the aero-drome here became Training Base 345 for

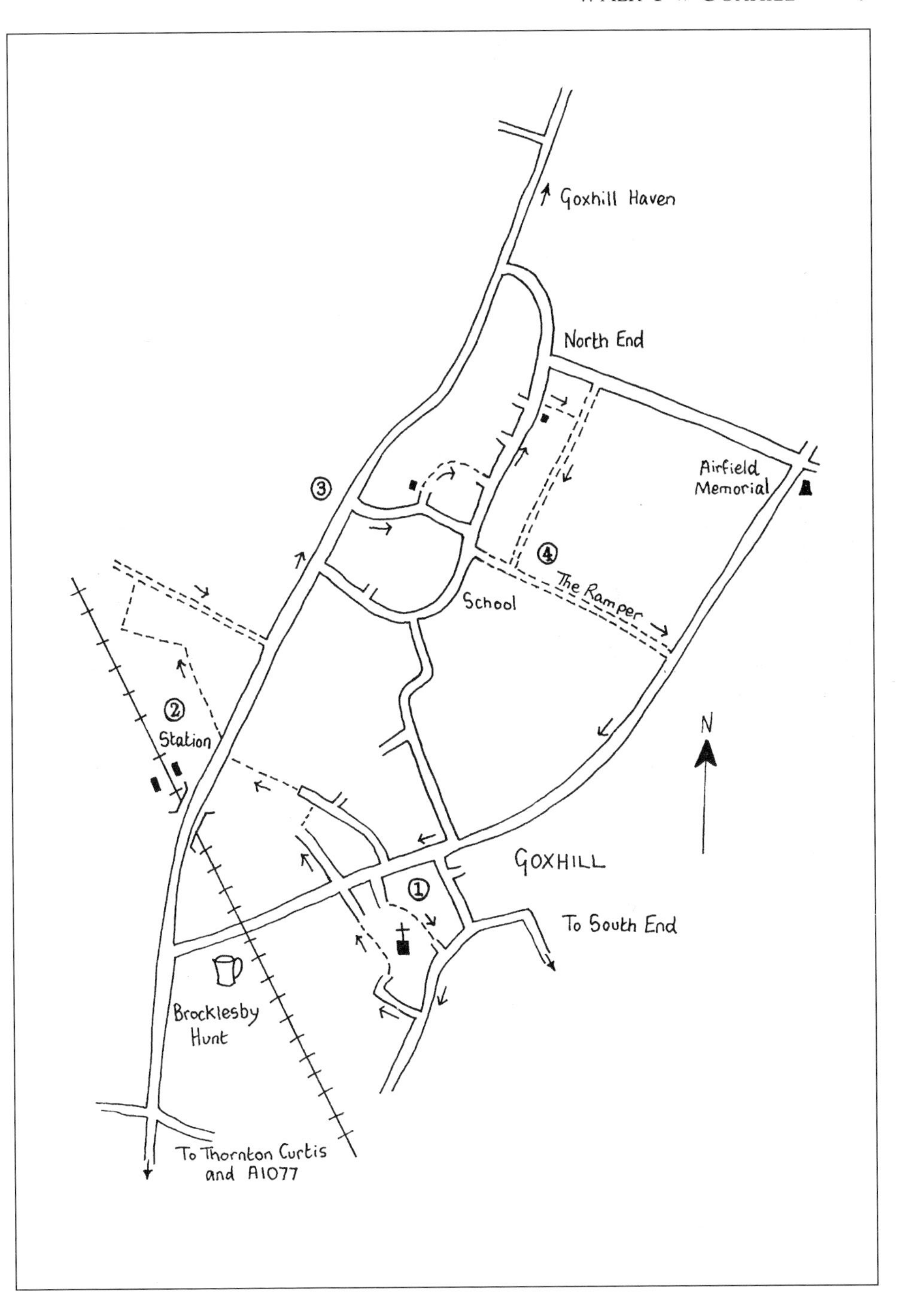

Goxhill Haven
North End
Airfield Memorial
③
④
The Ramper
School
②
Station
N
GOXHILL
①
To South End
Brocklesby Hunt
To Thornton Curtis and A1077

War memorial dedicated to a pilot from the USAAF whose plane crashed near the village.

fighter combat training with Thunderbolts, Mustangs and Lightnings, and a month before D-day a practice of the landing in France was held at Goxhill. An airfield memorial of a bent propellor boss, dedicated in September 1984, is from a P38 Lockheed Lightning which flew from this base and crashed in the parish on the 26th May, 1944. The pilot, 2nd Lieutenant L. A. Freeman, was killed and his memorial bears the following inscription: 'It represents the high price our countries paid for freedom'.

The massive church tower of All Saints is 15th-century and the porch doorway is well worth an inspection, having carvings of flowers and foliage, odd little faces and a quaint man. The church itself is full of light and there is an effigy of a knight in full armour who died in the second half of the 13th century. Don't miss the simple inscription telling the sad story of the children of Edward Skinner.

The railway station in the village is in the familiar Tudor style adopted by the Manchester, Sheffield and Lincolnshire Railway.

FOOD and DRINK

The Brocklesby Hunt provides simple bar meals and has some interesting maritime photographs in the lounge. It may not be open at lunchtime in the winter. Telephone: 01469 530468.

Goxhill Haven 2 miles from the village is the most northerly point of Lincolnshire and has a splendid view across the Humber to Hull.

PLACES of INTEREST

Only a few miles from Goxhill are the fine remains of **Thornton Abbey**. The abbey was founded by the Lord of Holderness in 1139 and after the Dissolution of the Monasteries Henry VIII held court there for three days in 1541. It once covered 100 acres and was surrounded by a wall and moat, the remains of which bear testimony to its former magnificence. Today the splendid gatehouse, built of stone and brick, is still standing 50 feet high and nowadays is in the charge of English Heritage. Telephone: 01469 540357. The **Humber Bridge** at Barton upon Humber has a viewing platform, car park and toilets, with an adjoining country park that is a most interesting wildlife area and the start of the Viking Way long-distance recreational path.

THE WALK

❶ This is a truly village walk and a most interesting one, exploring quite unexpected backwaters.

From the car parking space at the end of King Street by the splendid All Saints church follow the signposted footway with the church on your right and along Pigeon Cote Lane. Turn right at Churchside and right again, still on Churchside, taking a short path into Church Street. Cross the main road, now known as Howe Lane, to walk straight forward up Greengate Lane and onto a path at the end of a lane through a narrow kissing gate. Turn left to a waymarked stile to cross diagonally over the field to its right-hand corner where there is a stile and footpath signpost.

❷ Turn right along the road for only a few yards. Cross the road and go over the stile to continue on the signposted footpath. Walk diagonally right across the grass field to the metal fieldgate in the corner. Follow the track with the hedge on your immediate right and the magnificent Humber Bridge directly in front. At the end of the hedge turn right and walk towards the railway signal. There is a stile in the corner. Walk back down the track towards the village with marvellous views of shipping and Hull across the Humber. Go over an unusual metal stile and across the paddock to a similar stile at the roadside. On reaching the lane turn left for 500 yards.

❸ Turn right down Mill Lane with its bridleway signpost. Round the bend in the road just beyond Mill Farm turn left onto a signposted bridleway that is initially metalled. Follow the path round to the right to the road. Cross the road and turn left for just over 100 yards. Before reaching Ruards Lane turn right through a metal handgate to follow an attractive little path for a few yards to a stile. Turn right along the wide green lane for about 350 yards.

❹ At the path junction turn left on the signposted Green Ramper path with the primary school field and buildings on your right. On reaching the road turn right down Horse Gate Field Lane, becoming Howe Lane, and continue straight forward until you reach King Street and your starting place.

WALK 2

SCOTTER

Length : 2 miles

Getting there: Scotter lies on the A159, midway between Gainsborough and Scunthorpe.

Parking: There is a layby at the side of the river Eau at Riverside, among the ducks. It is directly opposite the White Swan across the river.

Map: OS Landranger 112 Scunthorpe (GR 887010).

Scotter is the largest village in North Lincolnshire and is situated on land that slopes gently down to the river Eau. A local historian suggests 'the mooring haven at the waters of the river roadstead'. An ancient canoe was once dug up at Scotter, hewn out of a large trunk 50 feet in length and 6 feet in width.

A settlement here was mentioned in the Domesday Book (1086) when two mills and two fisheries were recorded. In 1190 Richard I granted Scotter the right to hold a market and fairs, and the reign of King John gave it a confirmation charter and a visit from his Majesty in 1215. The King, trying to raise an army to repel the

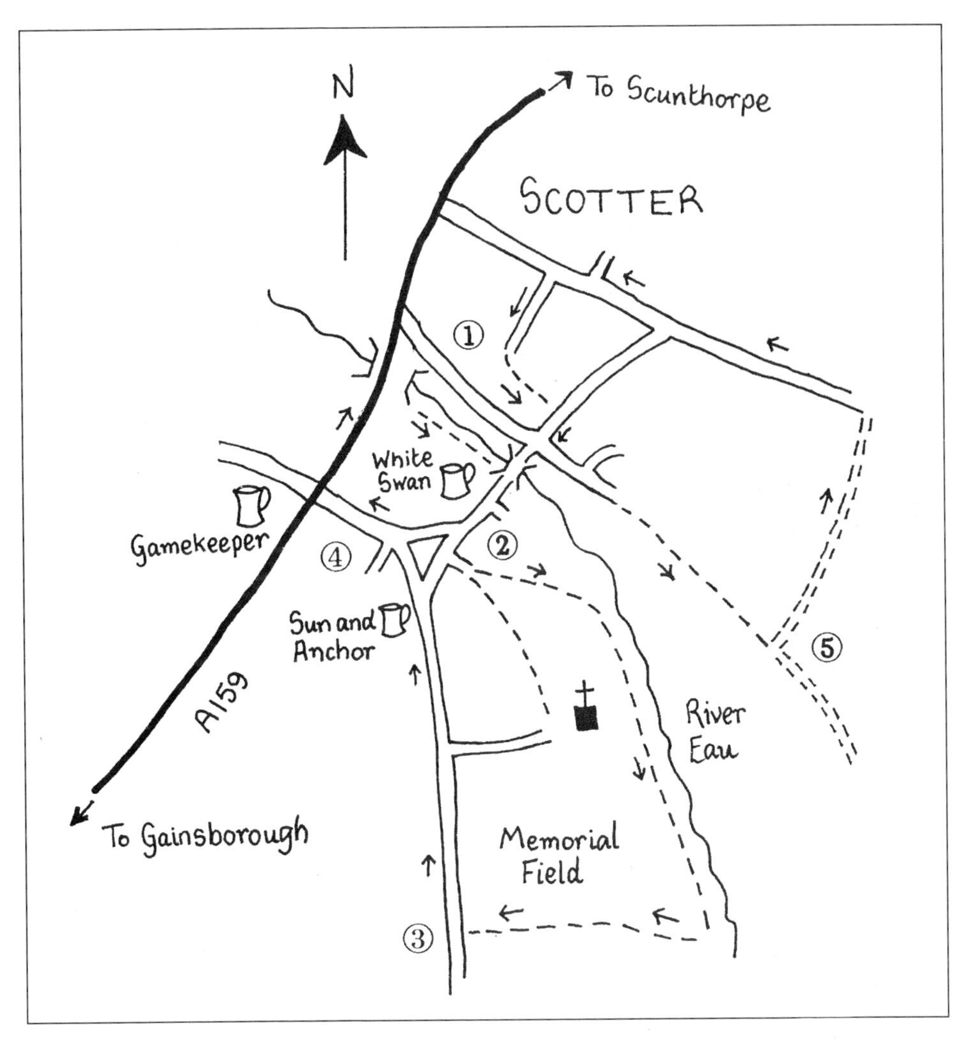

threatened French invasion, stayed in the inn facing the village green. The enterprising landlord, as a mark of honour to his distinguished visitor, redesigned his inn sign and incorporated the badge that was on the shield of the commanding officer — a sun and an anchor. The King is recorded as saying it would be good for the people of Scotter 'to have two holds — in Heaven and in the waters under the earth'. The present Sun and Anchor stands on the same site in the High Street.

St Peter's church was given to Peterborough Abbey by the King of Mercia in the 7th century. Above the present belfry door are the Ringers Rules in black and red Elizabethan lettering and memorial plaques dated 1599 and 1739. There is a complete list of rectors from 1125 onwards. Cromwell's soldiers are reputed to have stripped

Ducks on the river Eau at Scotter.

the lead off the roof to make bullets.

Between the two World Wars, swimming took place in the river between Scotter and Scotton, to the south. Nearby are two areas known as 'Big Mozzies' and 'Little Mozzies'. The origin of the names is obscure but they may have been corruptions of Moses in the Bulrushes. Big Mozzies was deep enough for swimming and Little Mozzies ideal for paddling.

The old manor house just across the river from the church is said, like so many others, to have an underground passage to the church. This fine-looking house is at the corner of Kirton Road and Riverside. The back wall of the house bears an unusual description, 'ANNO MUNDI 5710'. This 'Year of the World' dating was based on the Jewish belief that 4,004 years had elapsed before the birth of Christ. This therefore gave the date of 1706, though as the building shows signs of alterations and additions the foundations are probably a good deal older.

A short, easily walked circuit around an interesting village.

THE WALK

❶ From your parking place at Riverside turn left to walk along to the bridge. Cross the bridge and walk uphill with the White Swan on your right. On reaching the beginning of the village green turn left opposite the war memorial towards the church, with another manor on your left.

❷ After entering the churchyard turn left on well-used gravel path to walk steeply downhill to the stile. Continue straight forward at the first path junction and then left at the next path junction with the river Eau now on your immediate left. Some 500 yards beyond the stile turn right up the embankment to walk down the left-hand edge of the large War Memorial Playing Field. Go across the practice football pitch to the metal barrier onto a short track leading up to the main road.

❸ Turn right at the road, with the village hall and large car park on your right, to continue along the High Street. Turn right immediately past the village library down the lane leading to the signposted St Peter's church. Enter the churchyard at the end of the lane. Although the church is normally locked there are keyholders nearby who are only too pleased if someone wishes to look inside. Follow the path through the churchyard and upon reaching the road and village green continue towards the Sun and Anchor. Turn right upon reaching the main road and proceed along the High Street with Hobb Lane across the road on your left.

❹ Turn right at the crossroads with the Ivy Lodge Hotel on your right. Then, just before the bridge across the river, turn right down the attractive path, with the river now on your left. Turn left when you reach the road and after crossing the bridge turn right almost immediately up Clay Lane. Continue forward when it becomes a hollow way, avoiding Cherry Tree on the left.

❺ Turn left on a good track leading to Kirton Road and left again at the road back towards the village. At the road junction proceed straight forward up Gravel Pit Road to turn left down Colin's Walk. At the end of this cul-de-sac turn left along the path back to the road. Turn right downhill on reaching Kirton Road and thence back to Riverside.

PLACES of INTEREST

Gainsborough Old Hall, Parnell Street, Gainsborough is a perfectly preserved medieval manor house with original kitchens and a magnificent Great Hall. Open from Easter to October on Monday to Saturday 10 am until 5 pm, Sundays 2 pm until 5.30 pm. Admission charge. Telephone: 01427 612669. **Laughton Forest** and **Scotton Common** are only a mile down the Gainsborough road. There are some public rights of way but not unrestricted access. The hamlet of **Susworth** where the river Eau flows into the Trent is 3 miles away to the west.

FOOD and DRINK

There are three pubs in the village. The White Swan is very pleasant and has some rooms overlooking the river. It offers bar and restaurant meals and a genuine white swan. Telephone: 01724 762342. The Sun and Anchor, serving drinks only, is situated in the High Street. Telephone: 01724 763444. Both food and drink are available at the Gamekeeper, part of the Tom Cobleigh group. Telephone: 01724 762035. In addition, there is a licensed restaurant, the Ivy Lodge Hotel, on the route of the walk. Telephone: 01724 763723.

WALK 3

TETNEY

Length : 4 miles

Getting there: Proceeding northwards, turn off the A16 (T) Louth-Grimsby road at North Thoresby. Driving south, turn off the A16 just beyond Holton le Clay.

Parking: Authority has been given for parking at the village hall car park, at your own risk.

Map: OS Landranger 113 Grimsby (GR 315010).

The Romans built the first great barrier against the sea here and traces are still visible between Tetney Lock and Tetney Haven. Tetney is said to have once been an island and its ancient name was 'Teata's Island'. One local field is named 'Catchgarth' — the field where marauding Danes laid up their ships. The first church at Tetney was burnt by the Danes and the present church tower has scorched stones said to have been from the original Saxon building. On the subject of the church, Mathew Lakin, clerk and sexton, is recorded as having rung the bells for 84 years of the 19th century, which surely must be a record. One of the pillars in the south aisle

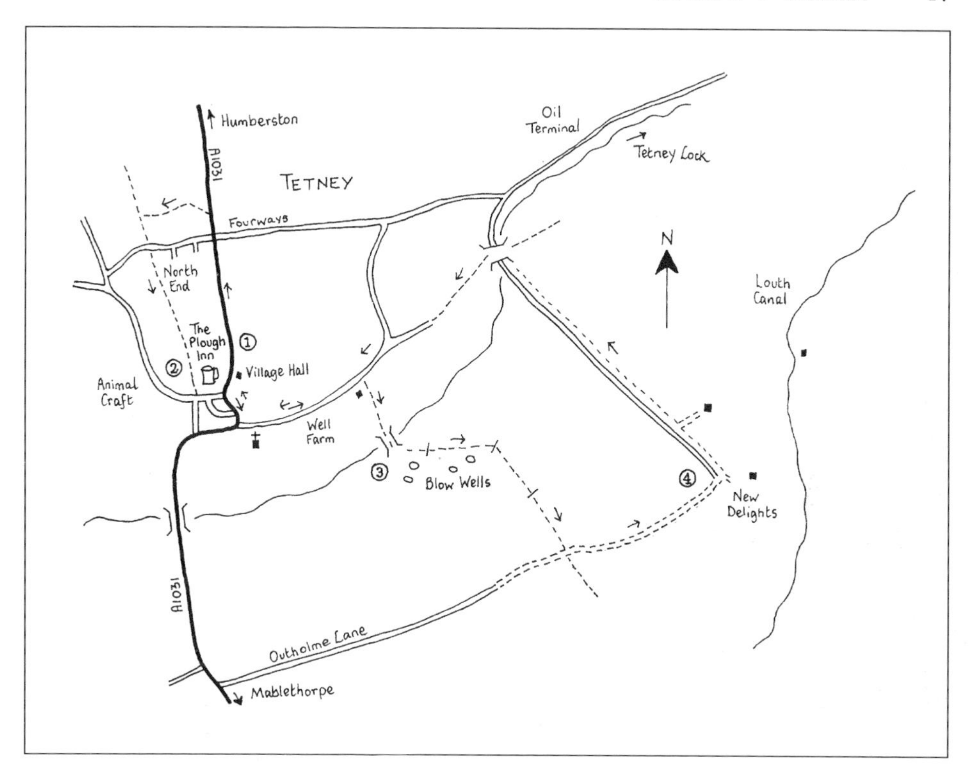

has a Latin inscription telling that 'the work was accomplished in 1363. Robert Day the vicar.'

In the first part of the walk, at North End, you will pass the farm where they raise polar bears! Animal Craft have a flourishing export business in otters, mice, polar bears and even Old English sheep dogs here. They employ up to 25 people at peak times.

Beyond the long stream from Croxby Pond, 1/4 mile from the church, are several blow wells. Common local knowledge argues that three of them are bottomless — and that the fourth is even deeper! There is also a persistent tradition that they are affected by the tides. In fact they are really springs of water rising from the chalk which is about 60 feet below the surface. This is the band of chalk that forms the Lincolnshire Wolds where the water table is at the height of 300 feet, so the water at Tetney is under considerable pressure. Heavy rain in the Wolds causes the pressure to rise about three months later, but it actually takes about three years for water that has fallen as rain on the Wolds to reach the surface again at Tetney. A sub-aqua club diving in 1961 found that the wells went down about 16 feet and, contrary to another local rumour, there wasn't a stage coach at the bottom. They do not freeze over even in the most severe weather. Today they are the haunt of wildfowl and part of a nature reserve. It is a secluded and beautiful spot.

The site of one of the blow wells that can be visited on the walk.

At New Delights the walk brings you very close to the Louth Canal. This was created in 1767 to link Louth to the North Sea by straightening the river Lud. The chief drawback of this 11¾ mile waterway, however, was the hazardous entry from the sea at Tetney Haven. In 1847, like many another canal, it was bought by a railway company to stifle competition.

The eight enormous oil storage tanks you see as you walk — they have a total capacity of two million barrels — are supplied from the Tetney monobuoy which lies about 3 miles offshore, the first to be installed in British waters. It is held in position by eight anchors and tankers are moored alongside and connected to it by floating hoses. Oil is pumped along a 36-inch pipeline to the shore.

Tetney Haven Bird Reserve, to the east of the village, forms an important feeding area in the mouth of the Humber estuary and a large number of wildfowl and waders may be seen on migration and in the winter. Gulls roost on the sandbars and skuas are frequent in autumn. The large breeding colony of the scarce little tern is of special interest and there are also significant breeding populations of shelduck, oystercatcher, ringed plover and redshank. So this,then, is a perfect walk for carrying a pair of binoculars with you!

THE WALK

❶ From the village hall car park cross the road with care because of the sharp bend and turn right to walk along the footway until 100 yards beyond Fourways. Turn left on a signposted winding, tarmac track and then left again at the path junction by the postbox. Follow this path in and out for 700 yards, including a short stretch of road called Stoney Way.

❷ On reaching the end of the footpath by the Methodist church turn left into the Market Place and then follow the main road round to turn left up Church Lane with the church of St Peter and St Paul on your right. After about 200 yards turn right into Well Farm Water Gardens. After your exploration continue up Church Lane for another 200 yards to turn right on a narrow, signposted footpath just past Tower Farm. Go through the gate and continue forward with the hedge on your right to the stile and good bridge over Tetney Drain.

❸ Follow the clear path down the embankment and across the paddock and, after the stile, detour to the right to have a look at one of the blow wells. Return to your path to turn right over a stile with the wood on your right. After another stile walk forward across the field to Outholme Lane. The footpath continues here to the Louth Canal but turn left along the unsurfaced lane and round the bend to New Delights Caravan Park.

❹ At New Delights turn left along a long, straight track with a wide grass verge and a large dyke on your left. At the bend cross the bridge and follow the signposted footpath on the left by the abandoned industrial buildings and then a small estate. This leads you to eventually rejoin Church Lane. Retrace your steps to the Market Square but stay on the footway of the main road round the bend to the village hall car park.

FOOD and DRINK

The Plough Inn in Tetney's Market Place is a friendly local pub serving hand-pumped Kimberley ale, but not offering food. Telephone: 01472 812319. Refreshments are available at Well Farm Water Gardens in Church Lane — an attractive place where you can wander over the extensive lawns and by the various waterways. Open every day between March and October from 9 am to 6 pm. In the winter (November to February) it is open on Wednesday to Sunday only, from 10 am to 4 pm. Telephone: 01472 814511.

PLACES of INTEREST

In Grimsby the **Back O'Doigs Museum** in Alexandra Dock is well worth a visit (allow at least 2½ hours). Open daily from 10 am to 6 pm all the year round. Admission charge. Telephone: 01472 344868. At **Alfred Enderby's** in Fish Dock Road you can see the traditional ways of smoking fish. Open all year. Telephone: 01472 342984. **Cleethorpes Coast Light Railway** offers a daily service (Good Friday until the end of October) from Lakeside Station in King's Road, Cleethorpes. Telephone: 01472 604657. **Waltham Windmill** in Brigsley Road, Waltham — to the west of Tetney — is open from Easter Sunday until October. Telephone: 01472 310661.

WALK 4

NETTLETON

Length : $2^1/_2$ or $4^1/_2$ miles

Getting there: Nettleton is situated at the foot of Caistor Brow on the A46 Market Rasen to Grimsby road, some 7 miles north of Market Rasen.

Parking: Arrangements have been made for free parking at Diatom International Sportswear Ltd at the top of Cook's Lane, Nettleton. This lane is directly opposite the Salutation Inn where parking is limited and restricted to customers.

Map: OS Landranger 113 Grimsby (GR 108003).

Nettleton — 'the farm where nettles grow'. The village is pleasantly situated on the western edge of the Wolds, at the foot of a valley a mile south of the Roman town of Caistor, and half of it (where you will walk) is in an area of Outstanding Natural Beauty. The weatherbeaten ironstone church lists its priests as far back as 1219 and the tower, except for the top stage and buttresses, was built towards the end of the Saxon period, with the doorway bearing the characteristic 'Jew's-harp' ornamentation.

In the late 16th century a large landslip

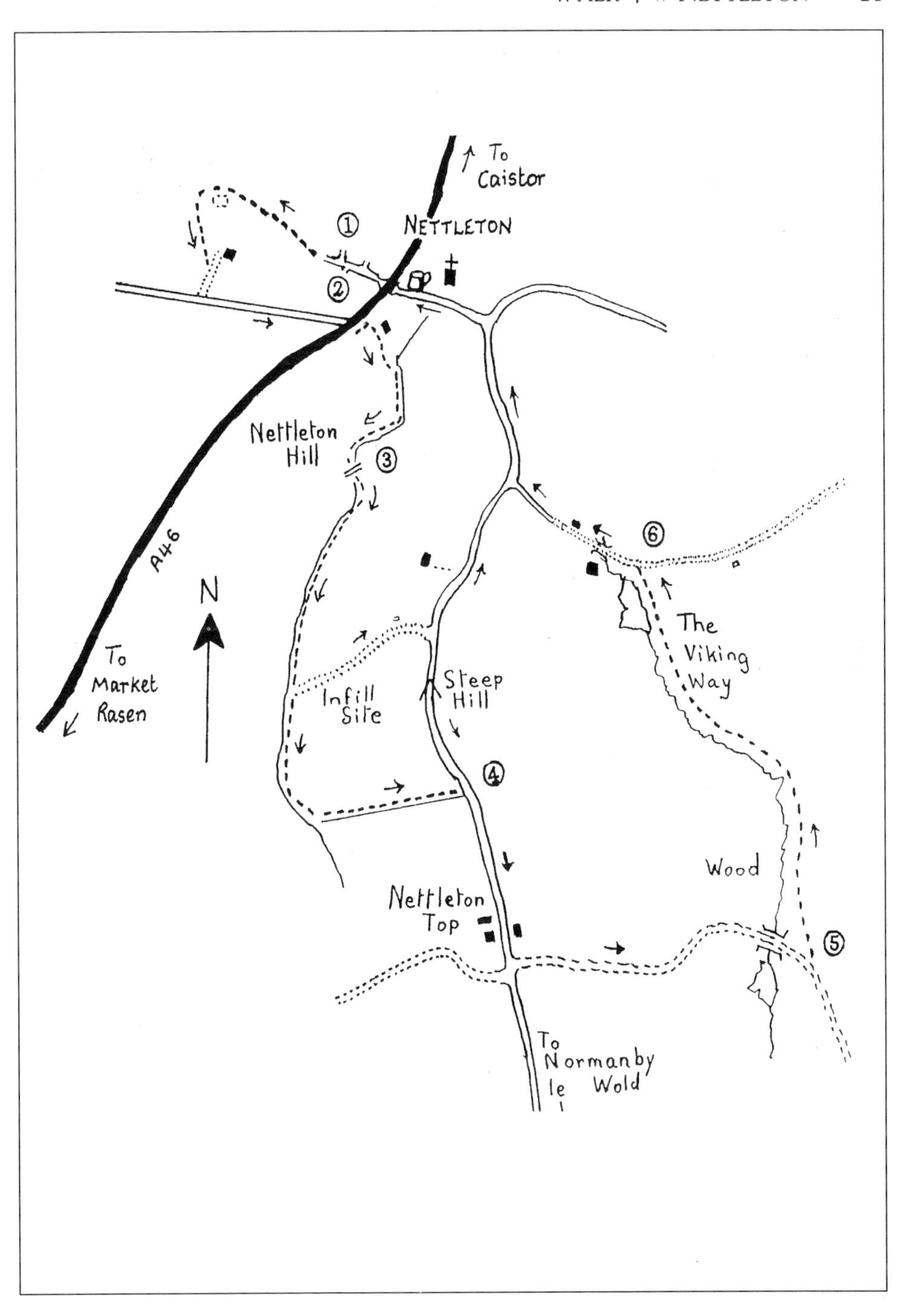
To
Caistor
NETTLETON
1
2
Nettleton
Hill
3
A46
N
To
Market
Rasen
6
The
Viking
Way
Infill
Site
Steep
Hill
4
Wood
Nettleton
Top
5
To
Normanby
le Wold

The Nettleton valley.

covered much of the medieval village, but pottery and coins from Roman times onward have been found during mining operations along the Nettleton valley. This was never an isolated community with its people cut off from the rest of the county, for its close proximity to a market town brought news, ideas and people into the parish. However, like many other villages, the appearance of the parish and the lives of the people changed dramatically at the end of the 18th century. It was then that Nettleton's open field and common pasture of over a 1,000 acres on East Field and the 1,100 acres of West Field were swept away by Acts of Parliament. As John Clare wrote:

Enclosure came and trampled on the grave
Of labour's rights and left the poor a slave.

An episode that does little credit to either the parish of Nettleton or its neighbour Normanby occurred at Kirton Lindsey Quarter Sessions in 1830 over the question of responsibility for the maintenance of a pauper. There was a ditch boundary between the two parishes and on a beam over this ditch was placed a bedstead. The pauper swore on oath that he only slept on one side of the bed in order to establish his parish!

Ironstone Cottage, the oldest detached house in the village was formerly the rectory. Methodism was particularly strong here and the Primitive Methodist chapel was built in 1858. It is now a private house, appropriately named Chapel House. Close to the old school a 'splendid designed parlour cottage' was opened by the Earl of Yarborough in 1922 as a fitting memorial to those who died in the Great War.

The climb up Nettleton Hill and the subsequent walk down Nettleton Valley must surely be one of the best rambles in the county and it certainly belies the myth that Lincolnshire is flat. The rugged hill-side gives a challenging steep climb and a rewarding panoramic view. Look out for orchids and wetland plants in spring and summer, as well as snipe feeding on the wettest areas.

A wide range of birds, many of them uncommon in Lincolnshire may be seen on this Stewardship land. In the marshy areas look for snipe, lapwing and woodcock; you may even hear the haunting 'cur-lee' call of the curlew. It is possible that you may encounter a heron fishing at one of the ponds or glimpse a kingfisher as you walk down Nettleton Beck. Birds of prey include the kestrel, sparrowhawk and occasional buzzard, as well as the rare and spectacular hobby.

FOOD and DRINK

The Salutation Inn commands the crossroads on a site where locals and travellers have probably sought refreshment since Roman times. This pleasing real ale hostelry is full of character and offers good value bar meals that change with the seasons. The proximity to Grimsby means that some of the fish dishes are especially memorable. There is a beer garden and a collection of farm animals to interest children. Telephone: 01472 851228.

PLACES of INTEREST

Horse World in Sand Lane, Osgodby, just north-west of Market Rasen, is an equestrian centre open all the year from 10 am until 8 pm. Riding instruction is available and there is a pets' corner and a cafeteria. Telephone: 01673 043407. The Forestry Commission's **Willingham Woods**, to the east of Market Rasen, are open all the year from dawn until dusk. There are colour-coded, waymarked walks, a car park and toilets. Telephone: 01673 844821.

The Viking Way long-distance recreational path from Barton upon Humber to Oakham, Rutland goes up the Nettleton valley and it is certainly one of the most attractive sections of the whole route.

THE WALK

❶ On leaving the Diatom car park turn right and keep straight forward on reaching the farm entrance on your left to a stile behind the little hut. Cross the field for a hundred yards to a good bridge with handrail hidden in the dip. After crossing this bridge walk to the stile on the right of the fenced enclosure. Turn left on the farm track down to the road where it is often muddy at the entrance. Turn left for 200 yards to the main road.

❷ Cross the main road with care, and climb the stile directly opposite. Follow the clear path round the field edge to the left until you reach the stile. Cross the stile and aim diagonally right uphill on this Steward-ship land until you reach the prominent signpost at the top. Walk along the hill away from the village with the fence/hedge on your left until you meet the first stile on your left. This is about $^{1}/_{2}$ mile from the direction post. Cross the stile onto the track.

❸ For the shorter walk you may follow this Stewardship track all the way down to the road with the infill site on your right and then turn downhill back into the village, although it would be a pity to do so. Or you can walk down this track and climb steeply uphill on the lane. However, you may walk straight forward on the negotiated permissive path for about 700 yards to the next Stewardship site field. Turn left at the far end of this field with the fence on your immediate right. Continue to the roadside where there is a fieldgate with a stile and map at the side.

❹ Turn right uphill along the lane. Continue up the road to Nettleton Top and just beyond the farm buildings on the left turn left down a signposted concrete path. There is a metal gate, a stile and a map here. This is the now abandoned quarry road and yet again Stewardship land. There are some fine views on the way down to Nettleton Beck and the ponds.

❺ One third of the way up from the pond overflow turn left down the valley on the signposted path of the Viking Way keeping the beck and eventually another pond on your left.

❻ Turn left on meeting the track crossing your front. Go over the memorial stile and read the inscription to my friend Nev Cole and walk down to the road with the farmhouse on your left. Turn right at the road back into the village, keeping left at the junction and walk past the weather-beaten church to the Salutation Inn and your starting place across the main road.

WALK 5

WILLOUGHTON

Length : 3½ miles

Getting there: Turn downhill off the B1398 Lincoln–Kirton in Lindsey road to reach Willoughton village. The turn is 2 miles north of the A631 Harpswell roundabout, 3½ miles from Kirton Lindsey.

Parking: There is a car park at the Stirrup Inn in Templefield Road, or alternatively you may find space a few yards further along by the bus shelter in the village square.

Map: OS Landranger 112 Scunthorpe (GR 930932).

Willoughton is one of a whole series of spring-line (the junction of the limestone and the underlying clay) villages that lie half way down 'the cliff' below the great prehistoric track, the Jurassic Ridgeway, that runs all the way between the south-west of England and Yorkshire.

Many of the villages along the cliff have early-Saxon names and, at a later date, were inhabited by marauding Danes who had ventured up the river Trent a few miles away. Willoughton means 'the settlement amongst the willows' and the willow trees at the end of Templefield Road must be

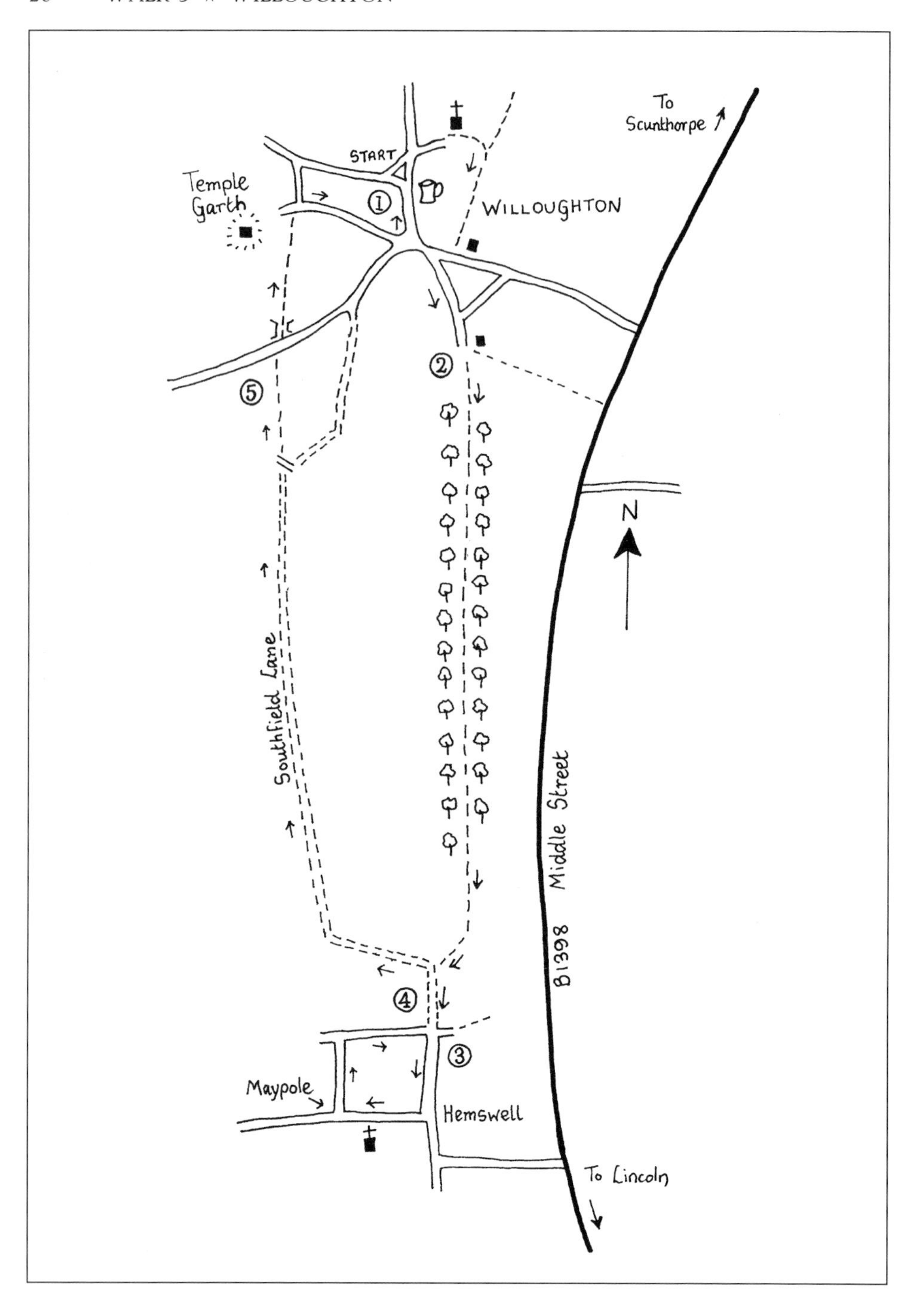
To Scunthorpe
START
Temple Garth
1
WILLOUGHTON
2
5
N
Southfield Lane
Middle Street
B1398
4
3
Maypole
Hemswell
To Lincoln

The village pub.

some of the largest in the county.

Willoughton was the site of one of the houses of the Knights Templars until their disbandment on the order of Edward II in 1312. In 1275 the brethren of the preceptory were accused of extending their rights without full warrant and 'raising a wall on the King's highway', possibly on Long Lane leading to Hemswell.

Enjoy a walk full of surprises through the Swineyard. This easy, historic walk on level ground begins in Willoughton village sheltering under 'the cliff', known hereabouts as 'the backbone of England'. It takes you mainly by long-used routes, past old moats and other ancient remains of far-off days to Maypole Street, in the neighbouring village of Hemswell. A good track then leads you across the fields known locally as 'the prairie' to the lovely trees overhanging ditches around Temple Garth, all that remains of the once proud preceptory of the Knights Templars, once so powerful in these parts. You may also see racehorses being exercised en route.

THE WALK

❶ Turn right out of the pub car park and, in a few yards, right again at the bus shelter to go down Church Street to St Andrew's church. Go through the elaborate wrought iron gateway into the churchyard and follow the flagged path past the church down to a kissing gate. The beautifully kept church has a real curiosity — a vamping horn, one of the earliest loudspeakers. Its humming note, said to be audible a mile away, called people from the fields to worship.

Go through the kissing gate and turn right with the boundary on your immediate right. The field is named Swineyard and the remains of moats seen here mark the site of a priory that once belonged to an abbey in France.

At the end of the field by the barn there is an old kissing gate leading onto Hollowgate Hill. Cross the road and proceed up Long Lane.

❷ At the end of the tarmac section of Long Lane proceed straight forward through the belt of trees on a clear track that may be muddy at times. Cross the grass paddock, over two stiles, and on joining the track by the three-fingered signpost turn left into Hemswell village.

❸ Proceed along Downhill Lane for some 400 yards to turn right at Church Street down to the magnificent maypole topped by a fox acting as a weathervane. Turn right along the appropriately named Maypole Street and right again at Brook Street.

FOOD and DRINK

The Stirrup Inn, named because of the nearby stud farm and racing stables, is a very attractive low-beamed public house. It is open nightly plus lunchtimes on Saturdays and Sundays and no meals are served. There is a small but pleasant beer garden. The telephone number is 01427 668270. The landlord is happy for cars to be left on his car park by people visiting the village. There is also a village store opposite the bus shelter.

PLACES of INTEREST

There is much of interest in Hemswell Cliff, to the east of Hemswell. The **Bomber County Aviation Museum**, ex-RAF Hemswell, is open on Sundays from 10 am to 5 pm. Telephone: 01427 668809. The **Craft Centre** at Lindsey House contains workshops, an exhibition and a restaurant and is open daily from 10 am to 5 pm. Telephone: 01427 667066. At the Caenby Corner Estate on the edge of Hemswell Cliff you will find **Hemswell Antiques Centre**, housing 270 shops in adjacent buildings. Telephone: 01427 668389. **Mount Pleasant Windmill** in Kirton in Lindsey is also worth a visit. Telephone: 01427 640177. In the nearby town of Gainsborough you can look round **Gainsborough Old Hall**, a medieval manor house in the care of English Heritage. Telephone: 01427 612669.

❹ At the top of Brook Street turn left on the track where you entered the village. Leave your original footpath on the right and continue along this good track known as Southfield Lane. The fields here are known locally as 'The Prairie'. Where Southfield Lane bends sharply to the right leave the track and turn left on a signposted footpath with a pond and a small thicket on your right. Climb the stile and walk straight forward across the grass field to a three-step stile by the road.

❺ Go directly across the road where there is a ditchboard, stile, footpath signpost and a waymark. Walk straight across the field over the green mounds that mark the site of the Knights Templars' preceptory, Temple Garth. On reaching the fieldgate and signpost turn right down the narrow lane back to the Stirrup Inn.

WALK 6

TEALBY

Length : 2 miles

Getting there: Tealby is $3^1/_2$ miles north-east of Market Rasen along the B1203, the Binbrook road. An alternative is to turn north off the Market Rasen–Louth road, the A631, making first for Tealby Thorpe.

Parking: Parking can be difficult in the village. However, there is parking for a couple of cars in the small lane directly behind the church, and there is limited parking at both the pubs.

Map: OS Landranger 113 Grimsby (GR 158909).

Tealby, situated on the very edge of the Lincolnshire Wolds in an Area of Outstanding Natural Beauty (AONB) is one of the county's prettiest villages, and winner of the Best Kept Village competition on more than one occasion. The golden limestone of the cottages, the rare thatched pub, colourful gardens and the meandering infant river Rase with its fords make it an interesting and attractive place to explore, with fine walks for all seasons.

Under the name Tavelsbi, the village was mentioned in the Domesday Book (1086). Even at that time, a dozen water mills were

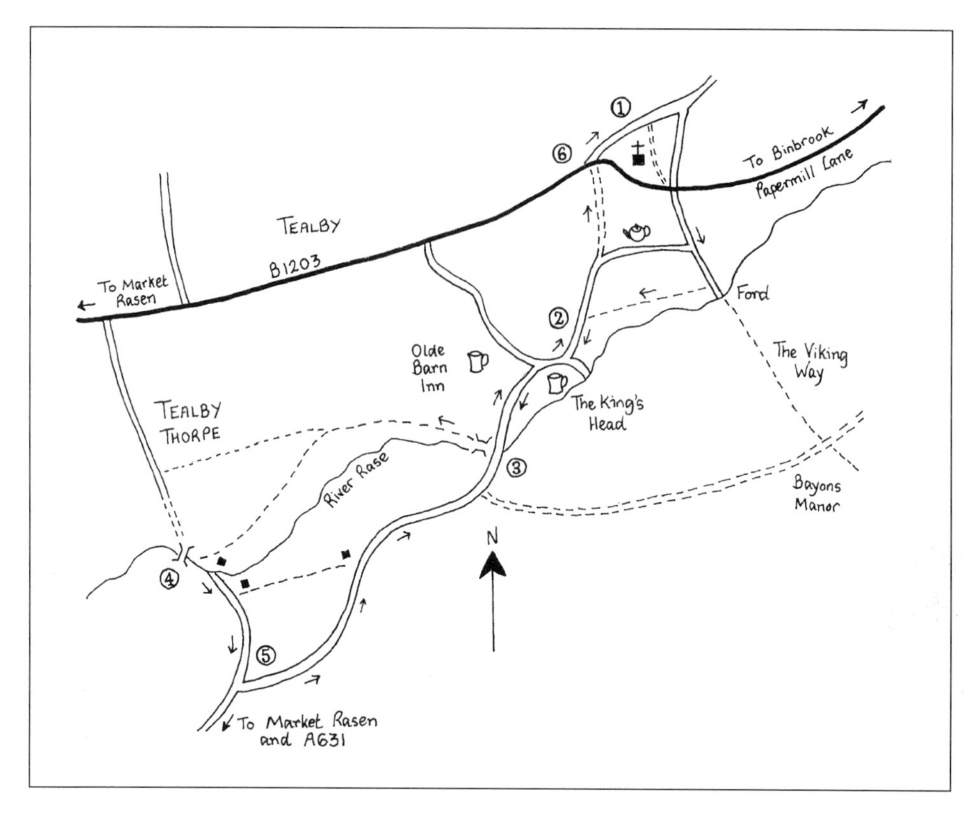

operating on land granted by William the Conqueror to his various knights in return for their service.

It was from one of these knights, Walter d'Aincourt that the Tennyson family, who were later linked with Tealby for many years, eventually claimed descent. The brother of William the Conqueror, Bishop Odo of Bayeux, was granted land here that eventually became Bayons Manor. George Tennyson, the grandfather of Alfred, Lord Tennyson, the Victorian Poet Laureate, purchased the manor at the beginning of the 19th century. The village still attracts people from all over the world through its Tennyson connections. Between 1836 and 1842 Charles Tennyson, Alfred's uncle, built a romantic Gothic castle, Bayons Manor, and added the name d'Eyncourt to his own, claiming a remote ancestor. Unfortunately the manor fell into disrepair after the Second World War and was finally blown up in 1964. However, the Tennyson d'Eyncourts left their mark on the village. Charles founded the school, a handsome building in the Gothic style, in 1857 although it was burnt down in 1889 and rebuilt the following year. Later, members of the family built the d'Eyncourt Memorial Hall which was opened in 1930.

One autumn morning in 1807 a ploughman trudging behind his team of horses on George Tennyson's land high on the wold towards Caistor High Street picked up a

The river Rase at Tealby Thorpe.

coarse glazed earthenware pot disturbed by the plough and found that it contained some 6,000 silver pennies of various mints from the reigns of Henry I and Henry II. It became known as the Tealby Hoard and some of the coins may still be seen in the Usher Gallery, Lincoln.

Another interesting connection is with the Knights Templars who held an important establishment in Tealby. The land behind the Olde Barn Inn is still known as Temple Garth.

At the very beginning of your walk pause awhile by the old stone porch of the church to examine the unforgettable view of the village below and the wooded countryside beyond, across the valley of the infant river Rase.

THE WALK

❶ From the parking place behind All Saints church go through the white metal gates and walk up to the church. It is usually open and is well worth a visit with its Tennyson connections, a simple Norman font, medieval beams and an altar table made from oak grown on the Bayons estate. From the old stone porch there is an unforgettable view over the hill with the school looking like a church, Bully Hill and, on the opposite slope, a magnificent stretch of countryside. Walk down the path and steps to the road. Cross the road with care because of the bend and walk down Beck Hill. The road on the left is still called Papermill Lane. Continue straight down the road, past the Memorial Hall to the ford with its Viking Way waymark and a signpost indicating 'Caistor High Street'. Turn back and 25 yards from the village side of the ford opposite The Old Cottage take the signposted path through the trees known as The Smootings. The infant river Rase babbles away on your immediate left.

❷ Upon reaching the road turn left to walk down towards the King's Head and to look at another ford. Return to walk along the road on your left for about 300 yards.

❸ At the third bend turn right off Sandy Lane onto a signposted footpath with a stile and a stout bridge with handrails. Turn left along the field edge with the stream on your immediate left. Over a stile and after the abandoned sewage works turn left again at a waymarked stile. Proceed diagonally right across the grass field to a waymarked stile and ditchboard. Go over the double stile to walk straight forward with the hedge upon your left. Turn left at the stile onto the lane with the ford and beck on your immediate right. Cross the bridge with the white painted handrails and turn left along the good tarmac track with the river now on your left and two attractive cottages across the water. This is the hamlet of Tealby Thorpe.

❹ By the ford turn right along the lane, keeping Thorpe Mill on the left. Continue up the lane to turn left at the T-junction.

❺ Walk back to the village on Sandy Lane, passing a pottery on the left, but instead of turning back along The Smootings path continue straight forward uphill on an attractive path that begins where Front Street turns sharp right.

PLACES of INTEREST

Willingham Woods, 2 miles away, is a Forestry Commission project with good parking facilities, ponds and many attractive pathways for walkers and horseriders. **Walesby Top church**, the unique ramblers' church in the next village, is another All Saints, which is not unusual for churches situated on pre-Christian burial grounds. It is always open. There is only a track leading up to it and in 1574 the rector left a sum of 6s 8d, the income from this amount to be used to repair the path. **The Viking Way** passes through Tealby and Walesby. This is a long-distance recreational path for walkers from Barton upon Humber across Lincolnshire, to end at Oakham in Rutland.

FOOD and DRINK

There are two pubs in Tealby. Real ale fans will find a choice of four excellent hand-pulled beers at the Olde Barn Inn in Cow Lane. Bar meals range from salads and sandwiches to Barn mixed grill, Tealby sausages, salmon steak and goujons of plaice, with a blackboard listing daily specials. Telephone: 01673 838304. The King's Head is a 14th-century thatched freehouse. Its two page menu includes home-made steak and kidney pie, chicken and ham pies, smoked mackerel and breast of chicken with an onion, mushroom and wine sauce served with rice. Vegetarian meals are also available. Telephone: 01673 838347. Home-made cakes, a selection of sandwiches and pots of tea are on offer at the Tealby Tea Rooms in Front Street, along with the possibility of a free talk on the history of the village. Telephone: 01673 838261.

WALK 7

FOTHERBY

Length : 2, $2^1/_2$ or $4^1/_2$ miles

Getting there: Fotherby village lies 3 miles north of Louth on the A16 (T) Grimsby-Louth road.

Parking: For the walk to Little Grimsby you can park just beyond the church by the old Sunday school building. For the walk to Fotherby Top turn westwards off the A16 towards Fotherby Common and park with care on the grass verge at the sharp bend in the lane, making sure that you do not obstruct the entry to the farm track.

Map: OS Landranger 113 Grimsby (GR for Fotherby church 317916 and for the lane leading up to Fotherby Common 310913).

This is an ancient place, for the Danes had a settlement at Fotherby and Roman soldiers previously passed this way en route to the important salt-pan workings on the coast. The village is less than 10 miles from the sea and the marshes around the Humber estuary and the beaches near Saltfleet later provided excellent landing places for smuggled goods from the Continent, either landed or floated ashore with the tide. The contraband then had to be transported inland, often at dead of night.

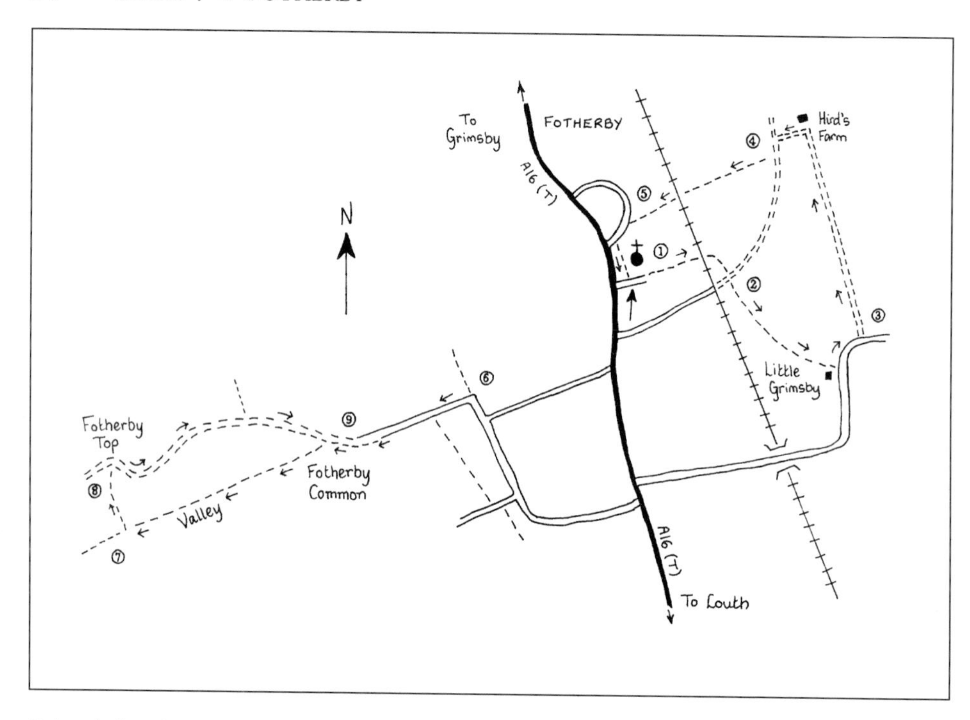

Behind the church, across a green paddock and half hidden among trees, lies a cottage said to have been a smugglers' den.

A church has stood here since the 12th century and the broach spire of St Mary's still dominates the village. The first known incumbent, Henry de Welton, received 6½ quarters of marketable corn a year, a silver mark and a penny for a marriage and a penny for a funeral. The church has a 15th-century font, three 17th-century bells and a medieval piscina with a deep flower drain. A monument like a scroll commemorates Thomas Jacob Freeth, 47 years a vicar here, who served as a chaplain to our forces in the Crimea. There is also a plaque to Colonel Cordeaux of the Lincolnshire Regiment, one-time High Sheriff of Lincolnshire.

Six almshouses have long been a feature of the village and although modernised internally their exterior remains unaltered.

The wooden toilet building in the bushes by the old Sunday school building, which is dated 1837, makes one recall *Clochemerle* for it was ordered to be rejected as 'unsuitable to the village' just after the Second World War.

Commons are rare in Lincolnshire and Fotherby is fortunate to have one situated high above the village. It is a pleasant place with newly planted trees, seats and splendid views over the marsh.

Most people drive through the edge of Fotherby on the busy main road between Grimsby and Louth without any excuse to turn off to explore. Here, then, are two contrasting short walks to remedy this. One is a pleasant, easy, low-level amble of 2 miles around the village itself and taking you to the hamlet of Little Grimsby with its splendid manor house. The other is an invigorating circuit of 2½ miles, starting on Fotherby Common at 350 feet and continuing to Fotherby Top. It gives panoramic views back to the village, and to the sea as far as the Humber and Spurn Point. The superb tower and spire of St James church in Louth may also be seen through the trees. To do both walks (a total of 4½ miles) would give you the chance to discover both aspects of Fotherby — and I'm sure that this won't be the only time that you turn off the A16 to enjoy this lovely area.

PLACES of INTEREST

Nearby **Louth** is a market town with a number of attractive hostelries and a splendid church. **Louth Museum** in Broadbank houses interesting displays of the past in town and country. Telephone: 01507 601211. Just south-west of the town centre is **Hubbard's Hills Country Park**, with good walkways around a river and steeply sided valley. At Legbourne, south-east of Louth, you will find **Legbourne Railway Museum**, a must for railway enthusiasts. Nearly 2,000 railway relics are on show, mainly of Lincolnshire origin. Telephone: 01507 603116.

THE WALK TO LITTLE GRIMSBY

❶ Starting by the old Sunday school building, go through the kissing gate with the well-kept cottage on your right and walk straight forward to a footbridge and gate. Cross the line of the abandoned railway, now a permissive bridleway, between the two white painted pedestrian railway gates to the lane. When the Louth railway line was closed in 1961, Fotherby was among the 17 stations that became redundant.

❷ Turn right at Peppin Lane for a few yards only and some 10 yards before the roadside railway crossing gates turn left through a half hidden kissing gate onto a signposted footpath marked 'Little Grimsby'. Follow this clear path round with wire fencing and a new hedge on your left to a footbridge and a stile with a waymark. Continue straight forward on the clear division between crops. The footpath becomes a rough track to pass by Little Grimsby manor house on your right. On reaching the road turn left for 250 yards.

FOOD and DRINK

Unfortunately, there isn't a pub in the village, but there is a general store — and a picnic lunch on the common between walks would work well. There are strategically sited benches among the young trees.

❸ Where the road turns sharply right continue straight forward on a signposted track leading to Hird's Farm with, at first, a tree belt on your left and later fishing ponds on the right. Upon reaching the outskirts of the farm turn left on a signposted diverted path with three small silos on your immediate left and follow the line of trees with two farmhouses away on the right.

❹ When you reach a track turn left for 70 yards and then go right at the first hedge, just before the telegraph post on your left. Proceed forward with the hedge on your right to the abandoned railway line. Here turn diagonally left across the field to a narrow concrete bridge over the beck. Walk straight across the paddock, with interesting hollows on your left, aiming for the telegraph post just to the right of the church spire. Cross the short marshy section with care to go through the wooden fieldgate onto the road.

❺ Turn left at Allenby Close to follow the road round the bend back to the church and an interesting wall. Walk through the churchyard to your parking place.

THE WALK TO FOTHERBY TOP

❻ From your parking space on the grass verge at the sharp bend in the lane from Fotherby walk uphill to Fotherby Common with its interesting sign. Continue along this good track for 150 yards after the final edge of the common to turn diagonally left on a clear, signposted path leading steeply down into the valley to the bottom left-hand corner of the field. Pass through the hedge coming down from the right and continue forward, keeping the stream in the valley bottom on your left.

❼ At the third large hedge, with its stile for another path on the left, turn right up the headland with a hedge now on your immediate left.

❽ On reaching the new barn go through the gap to the other side of the hedge and turn right with the farm buildings now on your right. In the field corner turn right through the metal handgate and, keeping the trees on your right, follow the grassy path, bearing right and then keeping the fence and hedge on your immediate right.

❾ At the shed go through the metal handgate on the right and turn immediately left. Continue for some 20 yards to join the farm track. Follow this good track back to the common and your starting place.

WALK 8

WILLOUGHBY

Length : 3 or $4\frac{3}{4}$ miles

Getting there: Approaching on the A1104, turn onto the B1196 in Alford town centre and continue for $3\frac{1}{2}$ miles to Willoughby, via Mawthorpe. An alternative is to turn off the A1028 Skegness road at Ulceby village (not Ulceby Cross), opposite the Open Gate Inn. Continue for $3\frac{1}{2}$ miles on a secondary road, via Claxby.

Parking: In the cul de sac by St Helena's church or outside the village hall in Church Lane.

Map: OS Landranger 122 Skegness area (GR 473720).

Willoughby lies in the Lindsey Middle Marsh near the eastern end of the chalk wolds. Its origin as the 'settlement in the willows' probably derives from the trees surrounding the springs that well up through the boulder clay from the underlying chalk in the vicinity of the church. Because the clay was difficult to work some of the ancient woodlands survive around the village, including Hoplands, which is now a nature reserve, and Willoughby Wood with its ancient heronry. In spring the 'heronsews' to give them their local name, are a familiar sight as they fly over

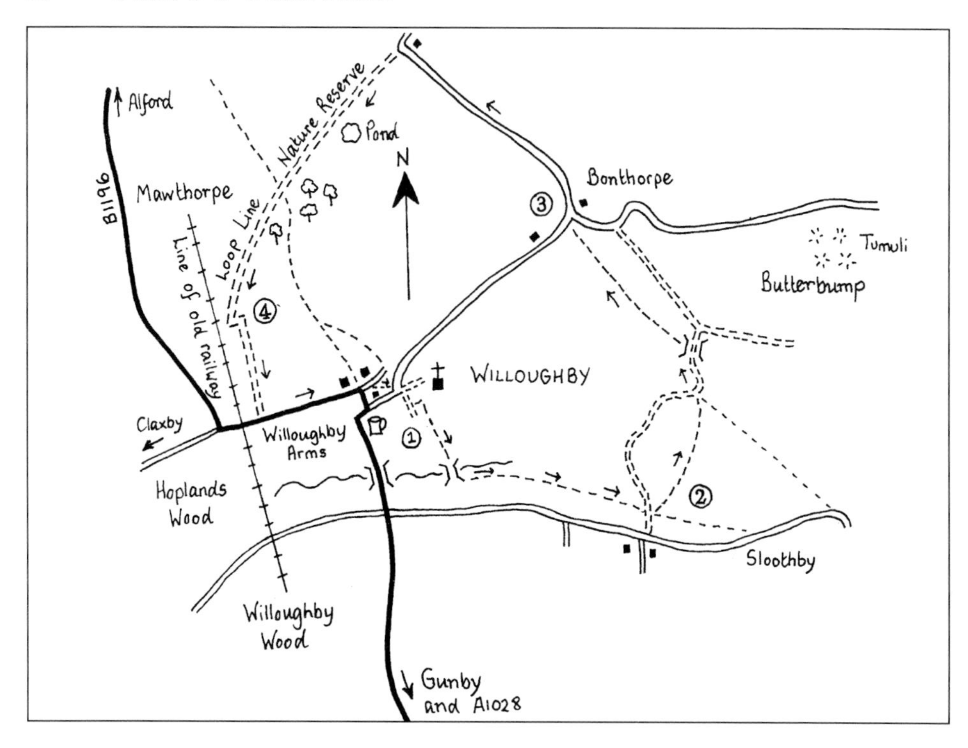

the village to fish in the marsh dykes.

Though the Domesday Book recorded a church here in 1086 the present one was built of local Spilsby green sandstone sometime during the 14th century. This sandstone is friable and prone to weathering so over the years the church has been patched up with varied brickwork. John Smith, the son of a yeoman farmer, was baptised here on 9th January 1580 and he later became Admiral of New England. The incredible story of being a slave, his life being saved by Pocahontas and some of his other adventures may be read about on the wall of the lounge in the Willoughby Arms. There is also a stained glass window in the church portraying events in his colourful career. The list of Willoughby's rectors dates from 1227 and one, Canon John Warren, retired at the age of 93 after serving here for 47 years.

Many people will connect Willoughby with trips to the seaside. On an August Bank Holiday as many as 5,000 passengers, mostly from the Midlands and bound for Sutton on Sea and Mablethorpe, used to change trains here at Willoughby junction. The signal box, tavern and station master's house have all become private dwellings and the footbridge that once went over the line is now in place at Burgh le Marsh fishing lake. The line was originally built in 1884 to connect with the projected fishing port and deep water harbour at Sutton on Sea. When it was eventually closed there was still no sign of Sutton Docks! 'On the 3rd October 1970 at 7.55 pm passed away after a long illness the Mablethorpe–

Willoughby British Rail Branch Line. Passed away but not peacefully.'

Since the railway line was taken up in 1971, however, the track has developed into a fine wildlife area with ashwood, hawthorn scrub and grassland supported by a varied flora. Butterflies include common blue and several species of skippers and browns. There is a good deal of bird life, including the occasional nightingale, and oak, field maple, birch and alder have been planted in suitable sites along the track. The pond, with an infrequent fisherman, is indeed a lovely spot.

This is a rural walk, much of it over fields, and some careful navigation is called for. You can choose to return to Willoughby by road from Bonthorpe — but this means that you would miss the delight of a stroll through the nature reserve.

PLACES of INTEREST

The 17th-century thatched **Alford Manor House** in West Street, Alford is now a museum and is open every day. Telephone: 01507 463073. **Alford Windmill** in East Street is open most Saturdays (also Tuesday, Friday and Sunday afternoons in July and August). It has five sails and four pairs of stones and worked commercially into the 1950s. In **Mawthorpe** there is a museum showing aspects of Lincolnshire country life. Telephone: 01507 463073. To the south of Willoughby, **Gunby Hall** (NT) with its beautiful old walled garden — reputedly Tennyson's 'haunt of ancient peace' — is well worth visiting. Telephone for details: 01909 486411.

THE WALK

❶ From your starting point in Church Lane turn right off the lane opposite the bend in the road leading to Bonthorpe. Go through the white painted gates to walk up the gravelled drive of The Old Rectory with the moat on your right. After 25 yards, just before the brick bridge, go through the white painted landgate and walk over the long grass at the edge of the graveyard to the small concrete slab bridge over the moat on your right. Cross the bridge and walk across the garden edge to the two-step stile. Go over the paddock, aiming slightly to the right to cross the fence and ditch. On entering the arable field walk straight forward, heading for the right-hand edge of the projecting clump of woodland. You will discover a stile and a concrete bridge with a handrail over the Burlands Beck amongst the trees in the left-hand field corner. Cross the bridge and should you wish to abandon the next section of the route a public footpath leads you straight forward to Mill Lane. Turn left on reaching the lane to rejoin the route at point 2. Otherwise turn diagonally left on leaving the footbridge, aiming for the right-hand end of the projecting woodland. Cross the ditch at the end of the wood, ignore the farm track and proceed straight forward over the field to an enormous narrow beam offering a temporary bridge over the drain. After crossing continue forward on the same line until you meet the good farm track where there is a half-concealed concrete foot-bridge and a gap cut through the hedge.

FOOD and DRINK

The Willoughby Arms is a pleasant Bateman's pub serving hand-pumped real ale and bar meals. It is often closed at lunchtime on Mondays. Telephone: 01507 462387.

For anyone who has chosen the alternative route this bridge is about 150 yards from the road.

❷ This good track goes all the way to Bonthorpe but it is not the public right of way. After crossing the narrow concrete bridge and going through the hedge turn diagonally left, aiming for the bend in the track some 800 yards ahead. Walk along the farm track when the footpath joins for 200 yards to a bridge with a concrete footbridge alongside over a very large drain. At the right-hand bend in the track the public footpath is left across the dyke and it goes up the field parallel to the track, with the large drain over on the left. The correct route is about in the centre of the field, halfway between the drain and the track. Walk straight forward to the hedge by the narrowing corner of the field almost by the road junction. It is possible to walk back to the village along the road from here but it would be a pity to do so for the best has yet to come.

❸ Follow the road around the bend with Wycombe House on the right at the junction and Bonthorpe House on the left a little further along Farlesthorpe Lane. After about 3/4 mile, where the road turns sharp right, turn left off the lane to enter the nature reserve along the delightful route of the old loop line. Pass the pond on the left — a good place for an apple stop — and Plains Holt Wood. Unfortunately, the two definitive paths south of the line are impassable and for some years there have been negotiations about an exchange in return for the connecting green lane but little progress seems to have been made.

❹ Go through the gate at the end of the loop line and turn left to join the 400 yards of green lane leading down to Station Road. Turn left along the road through the village and where it turns sharp right leave it and go through the kissing gate, then along the signposted path straight in front. Walk diagonally right across the paddock to a wide gap in the hedge and then diagonally right across the next pasture field to another kissing gate just to the right of the bungalow. Please replace the chain on the gate so that sheep do not escape. Turn right on reaching the footpath signpost on the roadside to return to your starting place.

WALK 9

HEIGHINGTON

Length : 3 miles

Getting there: From the B1188 Lincoln–Sleaford road turn off to Heighington at Branston crossroads. The village is about 4 miles from Lincoln.

Parking: Roadside parking is possible in Heighington High Street outside the village hall next to the Butcher and Beast.

Map: OS Landranger 121 Lincoln and surrounding area (GR 033694).

From the top of the village the towers of Lincoln Cathedral on its hilltop may be seen and down in the village itself the grey tower of the chapel at ease stands above red roofs. There are attractive stone houses and many of the narrow winding streets are lined with tall stone walls. Even new dwellings near the centre of the village blend in well with the older houses. Today there are two pubs in Heighington, the Butcher and Beast and the Turk's Head. In Back Lane there was once a third pub, oddly named the True Oddfellows. This may have been intended as a pun for I understood that Oddfellows were teetotal. There are certainly some other unusual

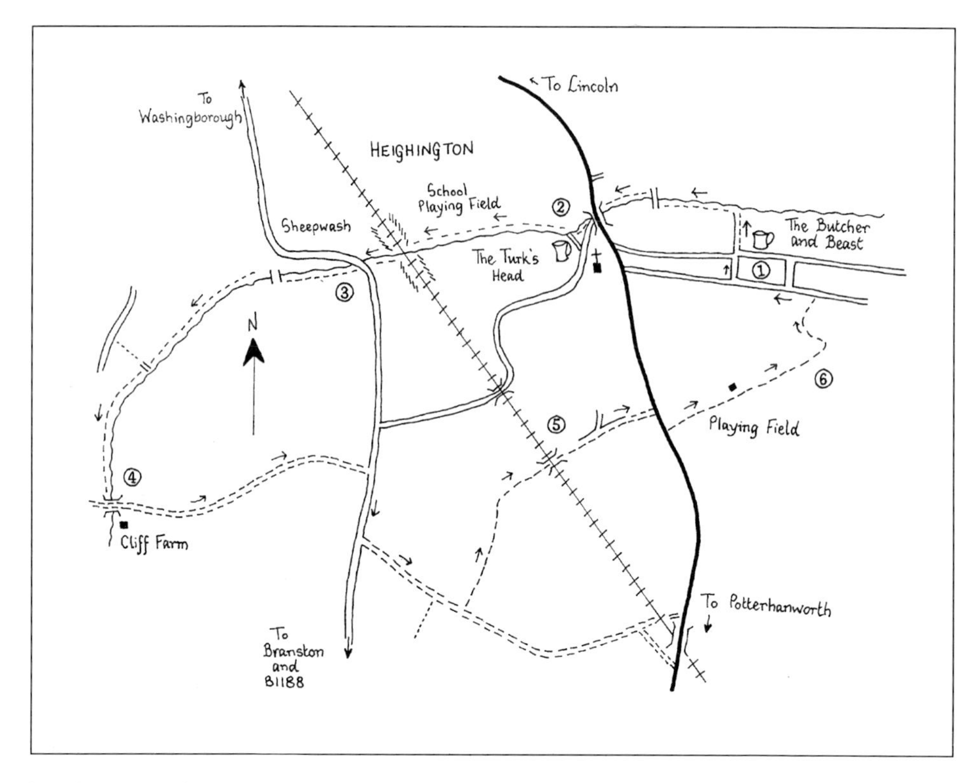

local names whose origins are difficult to discover, Pudding Busk Lane is one, another pleasant green lane is called Alaballa and there is Brinkle Spring Lane on the edge of the village. Park Lane, however, derives its name from the fact that the hill to the north was enclosed and emparked for deer sometime in the 12th century. The area by the road junction is known as Town End as the 'town' of Heighington stopped at Park Lane.

Not far down from the Butcher and Beast the High Street becomes Fen Road. The new house built there was the site of the village 'pinfold', the place where stray animals were impounded. If they were not reclaimed and the fine paid they were sold to defray the cost of any damage caused. Where Newcot Lane joins Fen Lane opposite the garage both hedges have been estimated as being 800 years old. Dating is carried out by counting the number of woody plant species, excluding briar and bramble, in 30 yards of hedgerow. The hedge after the sharp left turn at the top is much younger, only being some 400 years old. This puts it about the time of the early enclosure of village land recorded on 1st June 1575.

Deep ploughing on Heighington Fen, to the north-east of the village, has unearthed many trunks of black oak, thought to have been over 3,000 years old. It was known that there was a very early forest in this fen but when the climate changed about 900 BC peat formed by the increased

A quiet road in the village.

moisture choked the trees.

Thomas Garatt, who was connected with King Charles I's scheme to drain the fens, left a legacy in his will of 1619 to provide bottles of brandy and sacks of coal for needy villagers, and money to found a grammar school, 'proceeds of his land should be used to educate the boys of the village'. Today the distribution is a small monetary grant. He also left money to nearby Branston and Washingborough, but not to Canwick — allegedly because he was once refused permission to walk his dog in the churchyard.

One of the most attractive features of the village is the beck that flows through the centre and once provided motive power for the mill now converted for residential use. The walk takes one along the beck in the village and into the adjacent countryside.

THE WALK

❶ From where you have parked the car by the village hall walk past the Butcher and Beast to turn right down Blacksmith Lane, signposted as a footpath. Turn left on reaching the beck and continue until you reach the main road, changing sides as you proceed. Cross the main road to turn right along the tarmac path by the bus shelter with the stream now on your right.

❷ Cross the road at the end by the old

mill, now converted into dwellings, and turn right for only a few yards and then left between the buildings with The Watermill on your left. The public footpath is signposted at the roadside. Continue along the path with the school playing field on your right and the stream on your immediate left. Continue forward through the new development and up the flight of steps up the railway embankment and down the other side to the road and Sheepwash.

❸ At the sharp bend in the road climb the stile and continue forward with the stream now on your right. Turn left over the two-step stile and walk along the avenue of trees with the stream now on your left. Turn left over the next stile and continue forward alongside the stream until you reach the steps, stile and ditchboard by Cliff Farm.

❹ Turn left up the good track to the road. At the road turn right for 150 yards and then go left up the track with the curious name of Pudding Busk Lane. Some 300 yards along this lane turn left on a signposted public footpath across the field to the railway bridge.

❺ After crossing the bridge over the cutting continue forward with the hedge on your right (waymark) along the short track to the road. Turn right along the road for 100 yards and then left on a signposted path at the very edge of the playing field.

❻ In the corner of the playing field go down the steps and over the footbridge and continue to Almond Avenue. Turn left and proceed up Clarke Avenue to discover a made-up path leading downhill on the left towards the end of the cul de sac. Go down the steps to the road and turn left along this pleasant back lane. Turn right down Wheelwright Lane, the second lane along, and you are then back at your starting place.

FOOD and DRINK

The Turk's Head dates back to the 16th century and was originally called the Talbot. A bakehouse, brewery and stables once occupied the present car park. It is a Greenall's inn with hand-pumped real ale and bar meals are served most days. Telephone: 01522 790218. The Butcher and Beast, once the Bull and Butcher, was extended and modernised in the 1860s and is a friendly village pub serving both bar and restaurant meals. There is a pleasant hidden beer garden to the rear. The shape of the old building may be seen from the stonework of the side walls where they are not concealed by the many hanging baskets of flowers. Telephone: 01522 790386.

PLACES of INTEREST

Metheringham Airfield Visitor Centre, at Westmoor Farm to the south-east of Metheringham, houses a fascinating exhibition of photographs and memorabilia which recall life on the Second World War airfield of RAF Metheringham and the history of 106 Squadron who served there. Open April to October at weekends and bank holidays from 10 am to 5 pm. Telephone: 01526 378270. On the A15 Sleaford road, 2 miles south-east of Lincoln, visitors can watch the flying activities at **RAF Waddington** from a public viewing area. Admission free.

WALK 10

HAGWORTHINGHAM

Length : $1\frac{1}{2}$ or 3 miles

Getting there: Hagworthingham is on the A158 Skegness to Horncastle road, some $5\frac{1}{2}$ miles east of Horncastle.

Parking: There is a layby at the Horncastle end of Hagworthingham village at the side of the main road by a prominent telephone kiosk. Alternatively, the car park of the George and Dragon, in the main road about 200 yards east of the layby, is available for walkers who intend to visit the hostelry.

Map: OS Landranger 122 Skegness area (GR 344696).

Hagworthingham, sometimes called Hag, deserves better, for it is full of leafy hollows and narrow twisting lanes overlooking a beautiful part of the Lincolnshire Wolds. It is a delight and a place to remember.

Lord Tennyson, one of our greatest poets, knew the area well and nearby Stockwith Mill gave him the inspiration for his poem *The Miller's Daughter*.

I loved the brimming wave that swam
Thro' quiet meadows round the mill,
The sleepy pool above the dam,
The pool beneath it never still.

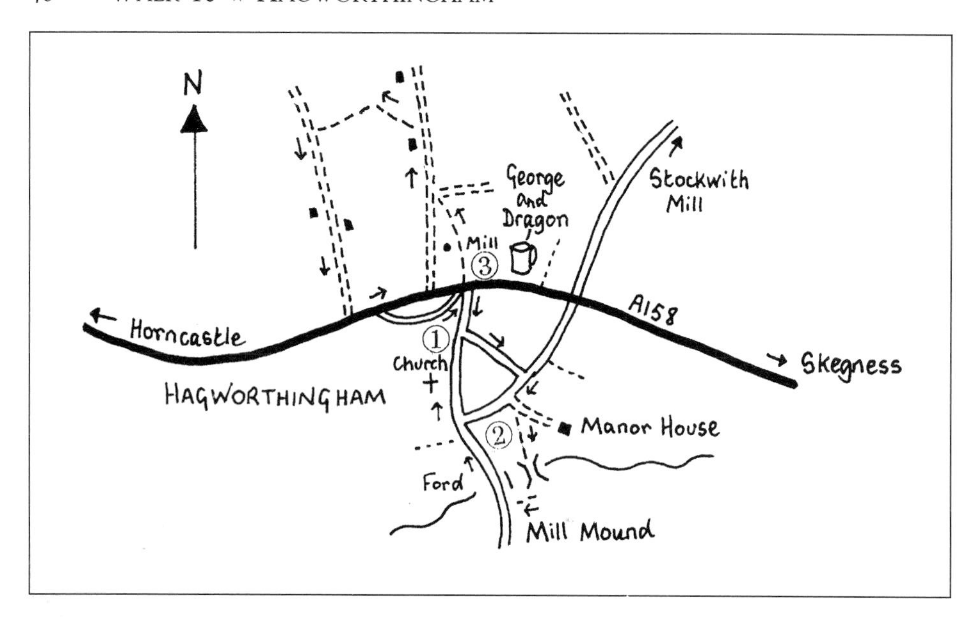

The infant river Lymn is considered to be 'The Brook' of the well-known poem, and Harrison Hall, a couple of miles down the road, now happily rebuilt after a disastrous fire, was the setting for *Maud*.

The seat at the side of the layby at the start of the walk is made of wood rescued from Holy Trinity church tower. The tower collapsed in 1972 and sadly the peal of eight bells was sold to Welbourn. The churchyard, above a hollow lane, is a beautiful place with some unusual gravestones.

Hagworthingham windmill is now capped and is a reminder of the Ellis family, who had a thriving milling and merchant business in the area. In Manor Road you will find the restored village pump. The Old Hall on the main road is an 18th-century house and New Hall next door on the corner of Church Lane is a nicely restored and well-maintained Georgian residence.

The walk through the village takes you down to a ford by a picturesque stream and nature reserve and then up a sunken road to the peaceful church and churchyard in a lovely setting. The second part of the walk goes by the old mill and down a most attractive hollow way to open fields with distant views of the Bluestone Heath Road, probably the most attractive road anywhere in the county. This is a figure-of-eight route with each loop being about 1½ miles.

THE WALK

From the George and Dragon car park cross the main road and turn right to the starting point at the layby and telephone kiosk.

❶ Turn down Church Lane with New Hall on your left, then go left up Bond Hayes Lane. At the road junction turn right along Manor Road. By the right-hand bend in the road walk straight forward up

The old mill at Hagworthingham.

the signposted track for about 30 yards and then turn right over a stile. Walk down the slope to another stile and then down to the substantial bridge across the beck. Go over the bridge and turn right through the nature reserve to the lane. Cross the ford by the small footbridge and walk back uphill into the village.

FOOD and DRINK

The George and Dragon, a freehouse in the High Street, is a traditional country pub serving fine ales and good food in comfortable surroundings. There is a beer garden and a large play area for children. Telephone: 01507 588255. Kelsey's Cafe is also in the High Street, just across the road from the layby.

❷ Walk up the slope off the road to the churchyard and church. The view up the valley from the church porch towards Lusby in the south is superb and just beyond the ford at Mill Mound was a far older burial mound. Turn left on leaving the churchyard, past the Quality Second Hand Shop back to the layby.

❸ On reaching the layby go straight across the main road, up the steps by the bungalow and along the half hidden, overgrown path to the mill. From the mill walk diagonally left down the field to the delightful hollow lane called Deep Lane.

Continue forward as far as Partridge Cottage on your left. Just beyond the cottage boundary climb the embankment on your left to follow the public footpath diagonally across the field to the signpost and stile in the left-hand corner. Climb the stile and turn left uphill to the left-hand corner of the next field and then go left on a good track with wonderful views, past the farm on your left and down to the main road. Turn left on reaching the road and continue along the footway back to your starting point.

PLACES of INTEREST

Stockwith Mill Tea Room and Craft Shop, just north of Hagworthingham, is open from March until December, 10.30 am to 6 pm. Telephone: 01507 588221. **Snipedales Country Park and Nature Reserve**, to the south-west, is open all year round and has picnic areas and toilet facilities. Admission is free but there is a charge for car parking. The remains of **Bolingbroke Castle** at Old Bolingbroke, 3 miles to the south, date from the mid 13th century and this English Heritage site is famous as the birthplace of King Henry IV and as the base for Royalist troops prior to their defeat at the Civil War battle of Winceby in 1643. Winceby is at the top of Snipedales Country Park.

Stockwill Mill.

WALK 11

BASSINGHAM

Length : $5^1/_4$ or $6^1/_2$ miles

Getting there: From the A607 Lincoln–Grantham road turn westwards downhill at Navenby, past the church, to reach Bassingham after $5^1/_2$ miles. Alternatively, turn off the A46 Lincoln–Newark road by Swinderby airfield, continuing to Bassingham via Thurlby.

Parking: There is a car park by the recreation ground, directly behind the primary school.

Map: OS Landranger 121 Lincoln and surrounding area (GR 905602).

This is a truly interesting village full of green corners, intriguing through ways curiously called jetties, attractive wall mosaics and historic old buildings — and it has a unique oak seat.

The splendid new houses that were subsequently built in Hallfield are also on the site of a medieval manor.

The Village Farmhouse, passed on the left in the High Street at the end of the walk, was probably built around 1796. You will see that some of the windows are bricked up and then painted to resemble windows. This was done to avoid payment

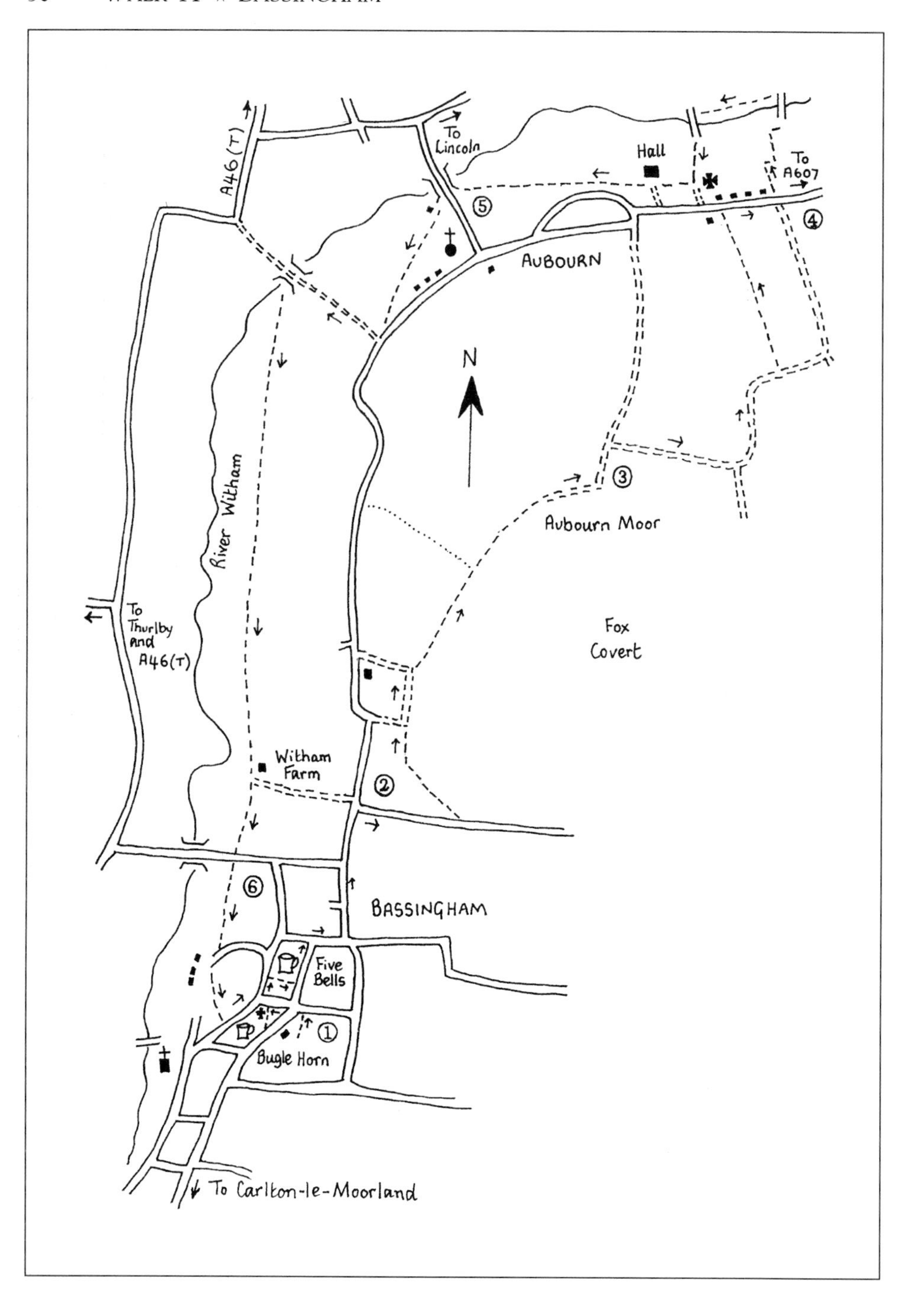

To Lincoln
Hall
To A607
A46(T)
⑤
④
AUBOURN
N
River Witham
③
Aubourn Moor
To Thurlby and A46(T)
Fox Covert
Witham Farm
②
⑥
BASSINGHAM
Five Bells
①
Bugle Horn
To Carlton-le-Moorland

This oak carved seat provides a welcome resting place near the end of the walk.

of the Window Tax, a tax that was only abolished in 1851.

An attractive walk, longer than some, but mainly on pleasant green lanes with good views on the way to Aubourn and then across arable fields close to the river for the return journey. The Witham bank is followed briefly, after negotiating an incredible metal footway that is supposed to be a bridleway on an iron bridge high over the river. A heron often uses the bridge as a fishing observation post. In pride of place on one of Bassingham's many little greens is a load of bull, perhaps better named Sitting Bull. The bull was carved in oak to make an unusual seat by a London sculptor, Mark Folds, in 1992.

THE WALK

❶ From the car park walk across the recreation ground towards the enclosed children's play area. After 130 yards turn left through the staggered gap in the perimeter fence, just before reaching the crossroads. Walk straight across the road and along the short tarmac corner path with The Hollies on your right. By the road junction at the end of Eastgate turn right down the High Street with Green's Stores opposite. On reaching the Five Bells public house turn right down the attractive footway at the side of the pub car park, Five Bells Jetty. Turn left on reaching the road and walk up to the T-junction. Turn right for 100 yards and then go left up Lincoln

Road past Badgers Oak housing development.

❷ Some 250 yards along Lincoln Road from the junction turn right down Fen Lane for 300 yards and then go left over the ditchboard on a signposted path. Aim diagonally left over the field to the stile in the cross hedge. Go over the stile and walk up the field with the hedge on your immediate right. On reaching the small thicket at the end go straight forward to join the RUPP (an unsurfaced public road) and continue forward on a good track. On reaching North Field Farm over on your left turn right just past the development on a signposted byway and almost immediately go left down the incorrectly signposted bridleway (this is also a byway). Continue forward on meeting a RUPP on the left until you arrive at a track junction. There is a good view of Aubourn church spire from here — there isn't a church attached though, for it burnt down. Turn right here for some 200 yards on a hedge-lined track and then follow the track around to the left.

FOOD and DRINK

Part of the building of the Bugle Horn pub may date back to 1654 when it was a town-house and stood in the middle of the road, and it is said to be haunted. Nowadays it is a pleasant and friendly traditional village inn serving John Smith's ale. Telephone: 01522 788333. The Five Bells pub is on the High Street. This has a restaurant and is low beamed, with lots of brass, some interesting pictures and a number of stuffed creatures, including a fox wearing spectacles. Telephone: 01522 788269.

PLACES of INTEREST

Aubourn Hall, passed on the walk, is open on Wednesdays in July and August, from 2 pm to 5 pm. Telephone: 01522 788270. There are lively forest walks to be had in the Forestry Commission's **Stapleford Wood**, 4 miles south-west of Bassingham. A little further south, in Old Sleaford Road, Beckingham, **Teddy's Farm** is open to the public from the beginning of April to the end of October, 10 am to 5.30 pm daily. It is also open at lambing time (mid February). Telephone: 01636 626557.

❸ On reaching the tarmac lane signposted Marlborough Farm turn right. (It is possible to shorten the walk here by walking straight forward into Aubourn but it would be a pity to do so. This would reduce the length of your walk by 1¼ miles. One could then rejoin the longer route at the public footpath just beyond the church spire). Where the farm lane turns sharply right after some 500 yards take the signposted and waymarked track on your left with a tree belt on your right. Where this good track turns sharply right after 500 yards take the signposted and waymarked public footpath across the fields. Aim just to the right of Hop Hill Farm now converted into a residence. There is a stile in the wooden fence at the end of a newly planted line of trees. Cross the small paddock to another stile and Blackmoor Road. Turn right here along the road for 150 yards.

❹ Leave Blackmoor Road by the last bungalow, with a byway sign half concealed in the hedge on the left. Climb the stile and walk on top of the bank. On reaching the river turn right to the high metal bridge. It would be a very acrobatic horse that could negotiate a passage over this bridge even though it is a bridleway. Cross the bridge and turn left along the river bank with the Witham now on your left. Walk along to the wide concrete bridge in order to recross the river. Climb the stile at the end of the bridge and walk up the field with the hedge on your immediate right, to another stile leading into the churchyard. The church, a lovely place, is normally open through the side door. On leaving the church walk down the marked path to the handgate, go across the estate yard and continue forward to the hall drive. Cross the drive and take the public path with the fence on the left and the tennis court on the right. In the left-hand corner of the hall garden you will find a double step stile. Follow the path round to the right, cross the barbed wire with its hosepipe cover and turn left up the paddock. Go by the metal fieldgate in the left-hand field corner, through the hedge on the right to a stile and signpost just beyond the new concrete filtration plant by the river bank.

❺ Turn left down the road for 200 yards and just past the former school, now a Heritage Centre, leave the road on sign-posted footpath with a stile. This path leads you diagonally left across two fields to the left-hand corner of the second field by the roadside. Turn immediately right down the unsurfaced lane signposted as a byway, as far as the weir across the river. Do not cross the bridge but turn diagonally left on a clear, signposted path to the ditchboard in the first hedge. Walk straight forward across the next field just to the left of the wooden electricity post. Cross the next small field to the signpost. Walk straight forward to the ditchboard and signpost and continue on this line over the next three fields to Witham Farm. Go round the hedge by the farmhouse to a stile in the left-hand field corner and then go straight ahead to another ditchboard and signpost. Walk forward between the trees to the handgate on the lane, although this is not a public footpath but a RUPP.

❻ Go straight across the lane over the stile, with the hedge on your immediate left, to another signpost and stile and then cross to the metal fieldgate on the right. Walk down the track to the road, known as Water Lane. Turn right and follow the bend in the road round to the left with Hallfield's new houses on the right and the river beyond. By Hallfield Manor gate continue forward on signposted path with a high wooden fence on the right. Cross the track leading to a new house, go over the footbridge with handrails and continue down the clear, narrow path to the road. Before turning left up the High Street cross the road and walk down to the junction by the war memorial. On the green opposite is the carved oak seat, with the church, the old Manor House and a path leading down to the river over the road. Retrace your steps back up the High Street, noting The Old Brewery and shortly afterwards the Village Farmhouse both on the left. On reaching the fine Wesleyan Methodist chapel turn right down Chapel Jetty with the Heritage Room on your right. At the end of this attractive path cross the road back to your starting place.

WALK 12

TATTERSHALL

Length : $2^3/_4$ miles

Getting there: Tattershall lies on the A153. It is 11 miles from Sleaford and $9^1/_2$ miles from Horncastle. It can also be reached from Woodhall Spa (4 miles), initially on the B1192 and then on a minor road, driving towards the castle that dominates the countryside.

Parking: You can park in Tattershall Market Place.

Map: OS Landranger 122 Skegness area (GR 212579).

Tattershall stands on the river Bain not far from its meeting place with the river Witham at Dogdyke. The first castle was built here by Robert of Tateshale in 1230. When Ralph Cromwell returned to England after Agincourt to eventually hold high office, becoming Chamberlain of the Exchequer, Master of the King's Falcons, Constable of Nottingham Castle, Warden of Sherwood Forest and Lord High Treasurer of England to King Henry VI, he transformed the castle into a magnificent home. With walls 22 feet thick at the base on the east side, the keep rises to 110 feet over four floors, plus two storeys of defence galleries at the top. In the great chamber on every level there is a splendid fireplace embellished with heraldic shields and

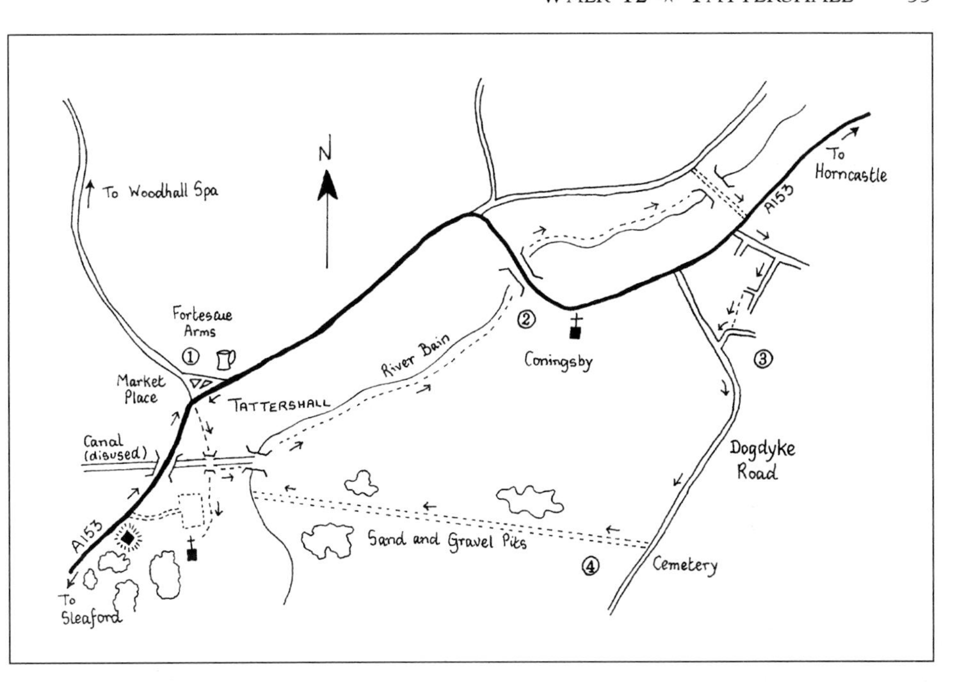

emblems, including here and there the purse representing Cromwell's office. The college buildings of Lord Cromwell's College, founded in 1439, which stood on the south side of the church have almost completely gone but the church survives in its entirety, except for its glass.

Lord Curzon of Kedleston saved the castle from dereliction when he bought it for the nation, only just in time though, for the magnificent stone fireplaces were already crated ready for shipping to an American buyer. Restored from 1911–14, it is now a National Trust property with a museum and shop in the former guard house. From the top of the castle you can see the whole route of your walk and, on a clear day, Boston Stump in one direction and Lincoln Cathedral in another. There is an unusual spiral staircase of 181 steps and the view certainly rewards the effort.

Close by the castle, Holy Trinity church is an enormous edifice full of light through some 60 windows. There are some splendid brasses. In 1989, at the 550th anniversary of this building, successor to an even earlier place of worship, a celebration was held and the great east window was restored. All the other stained glass windows had been removed to Burghley House and St Martin's church in Stamford, Lord Fortescue, the patron of the living, having given them to the Earl of Exeter in 1754, on condition that he reglazed in plain glass.

By the church are Bede Houses under one long pantiled roof, now occupied by six people but originally built to accommodate thirteen poor of the parish.

The Market Place, where the walk starts, has a 15th-century cross rising from four old high steps. Originally the right to hold a market was granted by King John, in

Swans on the river Bain.

return for a well-trained goshawk, it is said. Markets are not held in the square today. Tom Thumb's house may be seen on no. 13 on the west side — a reset 15th-century louvre in the form of a house with a door and window on either side. His 'grave' may be found let into the floor of the nave in the church: Tom Thumb, aged 101 years, died 1620.

This is an easy and interesting riverside walk over level ground to Coningsby, where St Michael's church is famous for its one-handed clock with the 16½ foot painted dial. Pre-mid-17th century, it is reputed to be the largest of its kind in the world and its unusual mechanism consists of hand-crafted iron wheels, stone weights and steel ropes. A Dutch national flag is draped behind the altar of the Royal Air Force chapel — this is the flag that a Dutch lady resistance member used to cover the bodies of three British servicemen during the Second World War. The route continues alongside Coningsby RAF Station, the base for Tornado fighters of Strike Command. Plane spotters often congregate around the perimeter watching aircraft landing or taking off from here. The Battle of Britain Memorial Flight is also housed on the airfield. The last leg of the walk takes you past flooded gravel pits, with opportunities to see a variety of bird life. Archaeological finds in the area's gravel pits include mammoth remains.

THE WALK

❶ From the Market Place walk past the old market cross with Lodge Cafe on your right. Almost immediately cross the main road to the attractive metalled footpath between houses 8 and 9, directly opposite Wayside Antiques. Cross the old wooden bridge and turn left down to the river Bain. Cross the metal bridge above the weir and then turn left to walk along the top of the embankment above the river.

❷ On reaching the road bridge cross the main road, left over the bridge. Then turn right through the metal kissing gate to continue along the good embankment path, but this time with the river on your right. When you reach the stile turn right over the little bridge to walk down the shady path called Masons Lane. At the main road turn right for a few yards and by the bend where you can see round the corner cross the road towards the Castle Inn after looking at Coningsby's famous clock with the RAF red and blue on the clock face. Walk forward up the narrow lane with the toilets on your right. Turn right up Fairfield and by the wall at the end turn left along a tarmac path and then right on meeting the lane with The Willows on your right. Follow the alleyway on the left to the road junction.

FOOD and DRINK

The Fortescue Arms in Tattershall Market Place is a typical old coaching inn, with a stable yard. It is a freehouse, serving mainly Bass ales. Food is served every day apart from Monday and Tuesday. Telephone: 01526 342364.

PLACES of INTEREST

Dogdyke Pumping Station, Bridge Farm, Tattershall is open from Easter to October on the first Sunday of each month, 2 pm to 5 pm. Telephone: 01526 342352. At **Tattershall Thorpe** there are two Woodland Trust woods with good walkways, near the Blue Bell Inn. The **Battle of Britain Memorial Flight** at RAF Coningsby includes the only Lancaster still flying in Britain. Open Monday to Friday, 10 am to 5 pm. Telephone: 01526 344041. At Woodhall Spa you will find the **Dambusters' Memorial Garden**, situated at the crossroads, **Ostler's Plantation** in Kirkby Lane, which has forest trails, and the **Cottage Museum** in Iddesleigh Road, open from Easter until October (telephone: 01526 353775).

❸ At the junction take the lane marked 'Dogdyke 1¾ miles' with the White Swan on your left. Dog Dyke Farm here has an attractive wind vane. Immediately beyond the splendid RAF playing field and directly opposite the beginning of the cemetery, turn right off the lane onto a good track with, after a few yards, a double metal fieldgate and a stile to the left.

❹ Walk forward towards the castle and the church with abandoned sand and gravel pits on both left and right. Turn right on reaching the river to walk along the top of the embankment until you reach the weir. Cross the bridge and walk towards the main road. Just beyond the old wooden bridge on your right turn left up the footpath to the Bede Houses, the church and the castle. Then turn right back to the Market Place.

WALK 13

HOUGH ON THE HILL

Length : $6\frac{3}{4}$ miles

Getting there: Proceeding southwards on the A607 Lincoln–Grantham road, turn off at Caythorpe to Frieston and then continue for $1\frac{1}{2}$ miles to Hough on the Hill. Proceeding northwards, turn off the A607 at Carlton Scroop to reach Hough on the Hill after 2 miles.

Parking: You can park, with care, in the mini-square by the post office.

Map: OS Landranger 130 Grantham and surrounding area (GR 923464).

The village lies on the edge of the cliff with a long S-bend leading up to the square. With a population of around 350, it must surely be one of the most attractive small villages in the county. There is a mini-square on top of the hill with stone houses, attractive red-brick 19th-century cottages built by the Brownlow family and an inn, appropriately named the Brownlow Arms.

The church of All Saints has a massive Saxon tower with a striking, rare outside circular staircase. The top of the tower with its crown of tall leafy pinnacles is a 15th-century addition, but the rest is Saxon. The whitewashed, atmospheric

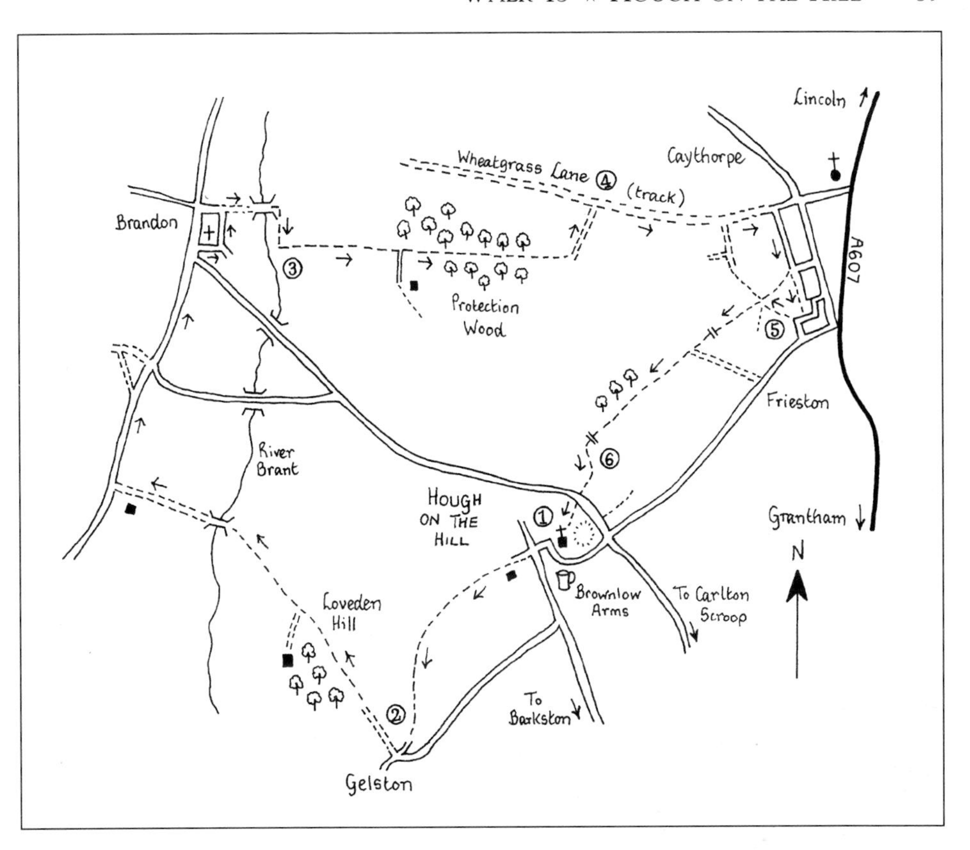

interior has a colourful mid-Victorian east window. The font is more than 700 years old and on the floor is a 14th-century gravestone decorated with a floriated cross. Near the church is an artificial mound called Castle Hill.

The beginning of the walk leads up Folly Lane with Hough Manor on the left. Hough Priory, of Augustinian canons, dating back to 1164, was demolished in 1983. It was one of 50 or so established during the reign of King Henry II 'to maintain divine service for the King and his family'. Its total complement probably never numbered more than one abbot and four canons and it was always struggling. By the mid-14th century almost everything had been sold to supply the monies due to the Royal Exchequer. In recent years the buildings in Folly Lane have been used to house cattle in winter. King John may have spent the last full night of his life here. John Betjeman wrote: 'stayed in a small priory at Hough-on-the-Hill after over-indulging himself on an unwise diet of peaches and new cider at Swineshead.'

The walk then takes you south on footpaths to Gelston along the very edge of the ridge with wonderful views across to the towers of Belvoir Castle and the Derbyshire hills. On Gelston green there are the remnants of an ancient cross on its

Brandon Hall.

massive base and steps. Not far from the village the infant river Brant begins its 10 mile journey to join the river Witham.

Loveden Hill, passed as the walk continues to Brandon, was an important pagan cemetery site in the period before the Angles were converted to Christianity. Later, in the Middle Ages, the hill became the meeting place of the local wapentake, a regular court holding local government meetings. When the site was excavated between 1955 and 1959 evidence was found of both burials and cremations from the 6th and 7th centuries. Some of the burial urns had the swastika emblem symbolising the sun or good luck.

This is an easy walk of contrasts, through woodland, along a hillside and over ancient tracks with some splendid views and a number of items of historical interest.

THE WALK

❶ From the mini-square walk across the road with the Brownlow Arms on your left and go up Folly Lane with Hough Manor now on your left. At the end of the track by the fieldgate continue straight forward (signpost) and contour round the field edge with a hedge on your right until you meet a stile and signpost after some 900 yards. Cross the stile and walk forward to another stile and then down into the dip to an earth bridge. After crossing the bridge over the small stream, turn diagonally left to walk uphill towards the white house with a wooden fieldgate and a stile on the right. Continue forward to the road, through another wooden fieldgate with a stiff spring bolt. Turn right to Gelston village green.

❷ From the green take the good track downhill on the left, skirting Loveden Hill, to cross the river Brant and continue to the road. Turn right on the road for 1 mile to Brandon and then go right to the church on the unfenced green. Walk up Blind Lane, right, for only a few yards and then left up Hall Road with the most unusual abandoned Brandon Hall on your right. At the end of the road turn right along the farm track. Cross the infant river Brant again and turn right with the river on your immediate right.

❸ After 50 yards turn left off the track up the edge of the field with the hedge/dyke on your immediate left. Go through the first cross hedge and at the bend in the hedge continue straight forward across the field to the edge of Protection Wood. Cross the old footbridge over the ditch with a signpost on the right to follow a good track with the wood on your left. Turn right for a few yards and then go left up a reasonably wide track with the wood now on both sides. At the end of the wood continue straight forward with the hedge on your immediate right, to turn left at the field edge with a coppice on your right. At the end of this coppice continue to bear left (waymark) with a fence on your right, until you reach a footbridge with handrail and signpost.

❹ Cross onto Wheatgrass Lane and turn right to walk uphill along this green lane. Continue forward past the new estate on the right to the grass triangle at the top of the slope. Turn right along Back Lane. At the left-hand bend in the road beyond the primary school continue straight forward between the houses on the signposted footpath. Ignore the right turning and go on until you reach the Millfield Crescent road sign in Frieston. Turn right here at the

PLACES of INTEREST

Cranwell Aviation Heritage Centre at Heath Farm, North Rauceby, off the A17 to the east of Hough on the Hill, houses photographs, exhibits and archive film recalling the history of Cranwell, from its origins as a Royal Naval Service Station to the present day. Open daily from 10 am to 5 pm between 1 April and 31 October, and from 10 am to 4 pm between 1 November and 31 March. Admission free. Telephone: 01529 488490. **Belton House** (NT), off the A607 just north of Grantham, is a fine Restoration country house, built in 1685–88 for Sir John Brownlow. Outside it has formal gardens, an orangery, landscaped parkland with a lakeside walk and an adventure playground. Open end of March to end of October, Wednesday to Sunday. Telephone: 01476 66116.

FOOD and DRINK

The Brownlow Arms Country Inn is an attractive stone-built hostelry with en suite rooms and even two four-poster beds. It is a friendly place and has a well-established reputation for quality home-style cooking and traditional ales. There are restaurant and bar meals but not on Monday lunchtimes. A pleasant beer garden lies at the side of the inn. Parking is limited. Telephone: 01400 250234.

T-junction with an attractive thatched cottage on the left. Walk forward for 100 yards before leaving the road.

❺ Where the road turns sharp left there is a step stile and a footpath signpost directly in front. Cross the stile and proceed diagonally right across this grass field to a stile, signpost and junction of five public rights of way. On reaching this stile do not cross but turn left downhill with the hedge on your immediate right. Go over the stile and walk down the field, keeping along the edge, then cross the farm track with Billy Roose Wood now on your immediate right. Cross the stile and follow the field edge round to yet another stile.

❻ At the next stile turn diagonally left to walk towards the church and Dyke Furlong Lane where there is a stile and signpost. On reaching the lane turn left to walk towards the church and at the grass triangle and road junction take the clear track uphill to the church. This path begins a few yards to the right on the junction. At the top of the track go through the metal kissing gate towards the old school with Castle Hill mound on your left. Turn right through another metal kissing gate into the churchyard and follow the main path past the church and down to Hough on the Hill square and your starting place with an opportunity for refreshment.

Folly Lane, Hough on the Hill.

WALK 14

BILLINGBOROUGH

Length : 3¾ miles

Getting there: Leave the A15 Bourne–Sleaford road at Folkingham, turning east past the House of Correction for 3 miles along the lane to Billingborough.

Parking: There is a free car park with an unmanned police box signposted on the right as you come into the village on the Folkingham Lane. From the car park there is a short alleyway leading into the High Street.

Map: OS Landranger 130 Grantham and surrounding area (GR 116343).

Here in Billingborough you will rediscover the timelessness of English village life — green pastures, sheltering trees, a Tudor hall, a lovely church and springs, bubbling up clear, cool and fresh from the stones close by the church. And, not far away, an even greater feeling of timelessness, of something truly rare and memorable — Sempringham. It is not in the centre of any village, surrounded by yew trees, attractive cottages, the village stores and passing cars. It is in the middle of fields, half a mile off the road, surrounded by potato fields, barley and oil-seed rape, standing splendid in its isolation. It is on a gentle hill, sharp and lonely as a lighthouse. And yet one

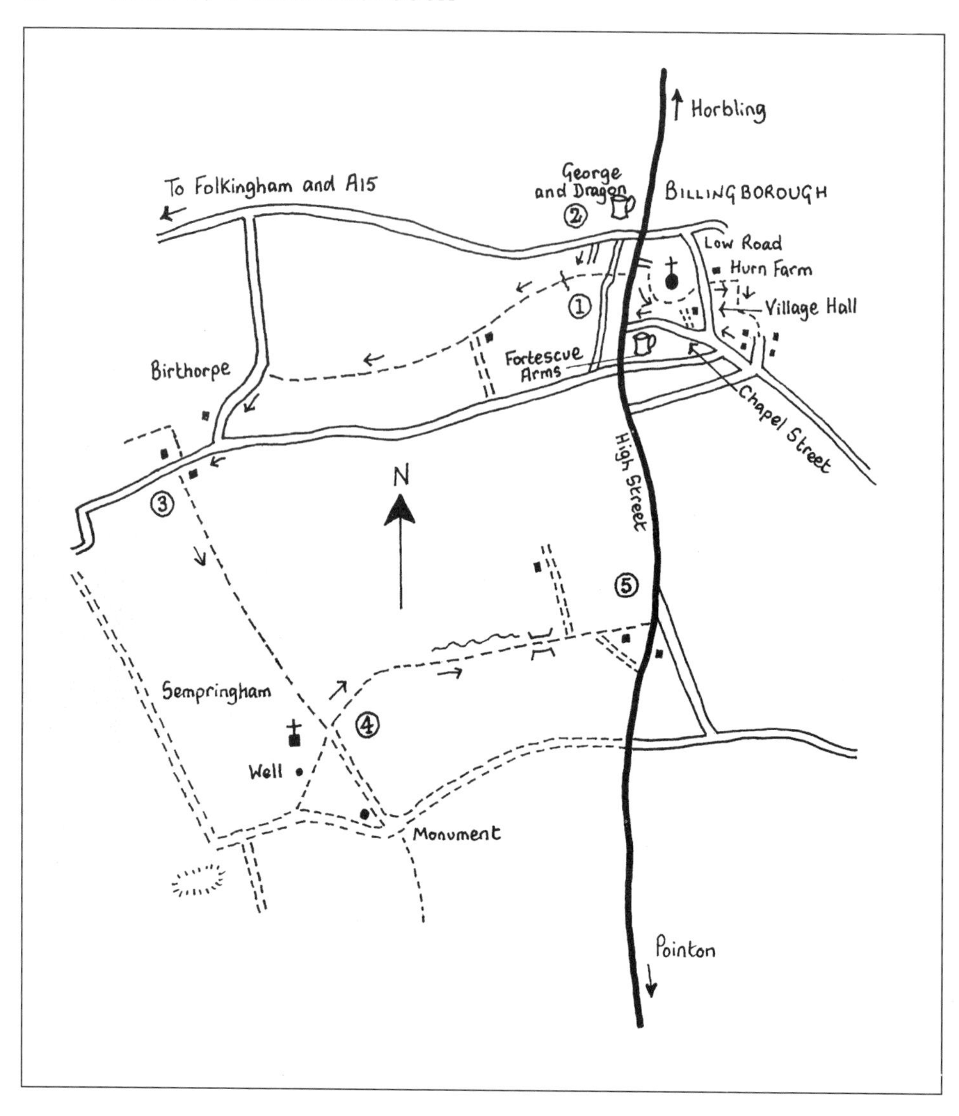

feels in a strange way that this site of a former priory is alive with people, for history has been made in this place.

Billingborough really means the 'burgh' or fortress of the Billings, a famous tribe of northern invaders belonging to the royal race of the Varini. It lies on the edge of the fen with the Roman Carr Dyke close by — more like a little town than a village, with its long street of houses, shops and inns and a lime tree avenue linking it to its neighbour, Horbling.

Hiding behind its wall and trees is a handsome hall of Tudor days with grey stone walls and tall chimneys. Nearby in a quiet byway is the church with its slender

The memorial to a princess imprisoned at Sempringham.

spire rising to 150 feet. Most of the church is 14th century although there are traces of earlier work and some fine glass. The east window of the south aisle has modern figures including that of Gilbert of Sempringham who was born deformed in 1088 and went on to found the Order of Gilbertines. The Winkley window commemorates 2nd Lieutenant Charles Reginald Winkley, Sherwood Foresters, killed in France in 1916.

The walk takes you over fields to the hamlet of Birthorpe and thence to Sempringham. Nothing remains of the priory today for at the Dissolution it was granted to Lord Clinton (afterwards the Earl of Lincoln) who pulled everything down and built a splendid house with the materials. This, in turn, was pulled down on the death of the second Earl in 1616.

Close to the site of the priory is a church a generation older — a lonely landmark among the arable fields with only tracks leading to it today. This is the parish church of St Andrew and its connection with Gilbert of Sempringham is demonstrated by an adjacent modern monument. In the far corner of the churchyard is the Holy Well, a peaceful spot. The moated area of the priory can still be traced some 350 yards south of the church. A monument nearby has been erected only recently to Gwenllian, the daughter of the last Prince of Wales, who was confined in the nunnery here at Sempringham from the age of 17 months for 54 years until she died. Her mother, the daughter of Simon de Montfort, had died at her birth. Edward I wanted the child to disappear and she could certainly never be allowed to marry and have children. In the flat fields of Lincolnshire she would not remember the mountains where she was born and almost certainly never heard her own language.

When the area around Sempringham was a deep fen prayers used to be said 'for the safety of such persons as had to cross so dangerous a place'. Happily your walk, although full of interest, will not put you in any danger today!

PLACES of INTEREST

There are forest walks and a parking place in **Callan's Lane Wood**, Kirkby Underwood. To reach the village go down the B1177 towards Bourne, turn off to Rippingale and cross the A15. **Heckington**, on the B1394 towards Sleaford, is another village well worth a visit. The Pearoom is the foremost centre for contemporary craft in the area, and the windmill is a unique part of Britain's heritage as the only surviving eight-sailer. It is a working mill on Saturdays and bank holidays from Easter to mid-September and on Sundays throughout the year. There is a small charge for admission to the upper floors.

THE WALK

❶ From your parking place walk towards the church via the narrow passage leading into the High Street. Turn right for 20 yards, cross the road and walk down Church Street. Unexpectedly you will discover the attractive spring and pond on the right with seats from where you may watch the ducks swimming across to their small island. Cross the church car park into the churchyard on a signposted public right of way. Just beyond the church porch turn left to follow a clear, winding track through the graveyard and on to the tarmac track leading to the road with the cottages on your left. Turn right along Low Road for only a few yards to Hurn farmhouse. Turn left here up a signposted tarmac public path and, at the end of the track, turn right over the bridge into the lane, oddly enough called White Leather Square. At the end of the lane turn right and proceed up Harpel Street, the second on the left, passing Arrow Travel en route. Turn left up Chapel Street, just beyond the village hall over on the right. The Fortescue Arms is on your left when you reach the High Street. Walk back to the car park and turn right along West Road with the fire station on your right, until you reach Folkingham Lane.

FOOD and DRINK

There are two pubs in Billingborough. The Fortescue Arms is an attractive hostelry with a pleasant garden containing picnic tables and a genuine — grounded — boat for children's play. Telephone: 01529 240228. The George and Dragon is a typical, friendly village pub. Telephone: 01529 240334.

❷ Turn left along Folkingham Lane for 100 yards and then left up the green track just beyond the old station yard and former railway. Upon reaching the footpath signpost turn right across the small field to a decrepit ditchboard over the first small dyke. Aim for the left-hand corner of the next field and just behind the house you will discover an earth bridge. Follow this dyke immediately on your left all the way until you reach the lane leading into Birthorpe. Walk forward into the hamlet, with the manor house on your right.

❸ When you reach the barns on your left turn left on a signposted path almost alongside the last barn, walking towards Sempringham church spire. On reaching the little copse of trees aim to the right-hand corner of the field to cross the dyke by another earth bridge. Turn left parallel to the dyke about 30 yards into the field. Continue forward in the next field towards the telegraph post in the trees, aiming for the end of the hedge where there is a ditchboard in place. Walk forward towards the church with the dyke on your right. Enter the churchyard and take time to look at the monument to Gilbert of Sempringham and the Holy Well, then walk down the track to contemplate the monument recently erected to Princess Gwenllian. Retrace your steps to the church entrance.

❹ From the kissing gate at the entrance to the churchyard walk straight forward across the field in a direct line to the telegraph post situated at the bend in the farm track. Walk down the headland with the hedge on your immediate left. Cross the dyke onto the track which is really a RUPP (road used as a public path). Continue straight forward amongst the farm buildings and equipment, through the white gate onto the gravelled path leading to the road. The path is (incorrectly) signed here as a bridleway.

❺ Turn left up the road back into Billingborough village.

WALK 15

FRAMPTON

Length : 3 miles

Getting there: Turn off the A16 (T) at Kirton roundabout south of Boston.

Parking: You can park near Frampton church.

Map: OS Landranger 131 Boston and Spalding area (GR 326393).

There are some fine trees in this fen village not far from the Wash marshes. They make a charming setting for the lovely old church, with Frampton Hall, a Queen Anne house in a small park, directly across the lane.

Frampton Hall was built in 1725 by Coney Tunnard and rabbits appear on many parts of the building and railings as a pun on his name. There is a rabbit on the chandelier he gave to St Mary the Virgin church which is normally open during daylight hours. Have a look for Richard-in-the-Corner outside on the gables buttress of the church transept and read the quaint inscription. The Moore's Arms, is named after Colonel Moore who lived at the Hall.

At Church End the imposing brick house with walled gardens is Cotton Hall.

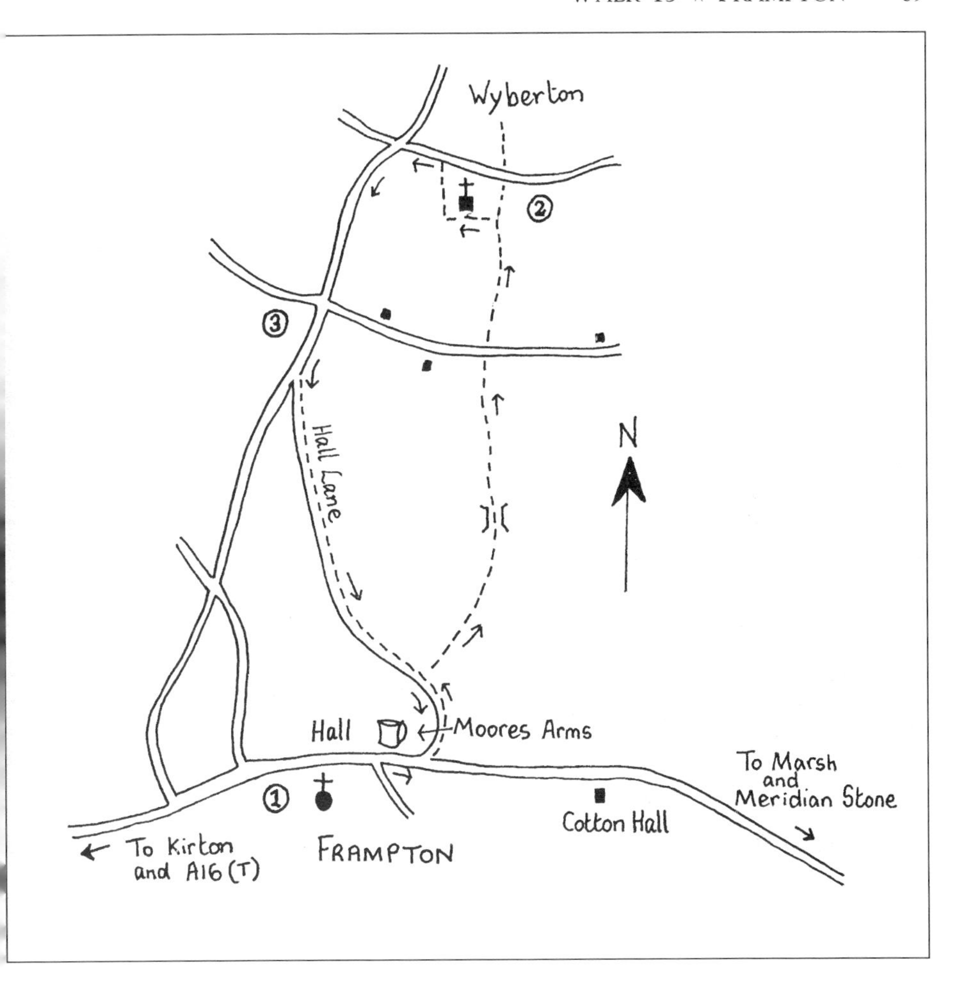

The Cotton family were possibly related to John Cotton, Governor of Massachusetts, who is commemorated in the Cotton Chapel at Boston Stump.

The Greenwich Meridian is crossed further down the road past Cotton Hall on the way to the sea banks and the marshes. Frampton Marsh is a bird sanctuary and it is here that samphire may be found. This is a local delicacy boiled and pickled in vinegar before eating with cold ham.

In Ralph's Lane, at West Frampton, you can see a sign headed 'The Gibbet Pit', erected by Frampton Parish Council in 1983. It continues: 'On this site in 1792 stood the gibbet on which hung the body of Ralph Smith, the last man in the Boston area to be hung in chains. He was accused of the murder of Gentle Sutton.' On extremely circumstantial evidence Ralph Smith was taken into custody on suspicion of guilt. He had just returned from transportation to Australia and became

The Greenwich Meridian stone.

an obvious suspect. Apparently the gibbeting was done at the request of certain persons in the neighbourhood so he obviously had enemies.

In November 1987 Lord Willoughby de Broke, who succeeded to the title on the death of his father the 19th Baron, a famous racehorse owner and breeder, sold the Lordship of the Manor of Frampton by auction. Actually there are three manors in Frampton and the Lordship offered was that of Stone Hall. The other manors in the parish are Earl's Hall and Multon Hall.

This is a pleasant, easy walk over level ground with some footbridges and stiles en route. Be sure to allow time to 'stand and stare'.

FOOD and DRINK

The Moore's Arms, dated 1690, with its low beams and horse brasses, is a very pleasant place to dine. It serves traditional, home-cooked fayre, with some original dishes like Farmers' Boots — deep fried potatoes with bacon filling. Whitebait, trout, lemon sole, Boston kippers and fresh Grimsby fish also appear on the menu. Telephone: 01205 722408.

THE WALK

❶ From Frampton church entrance walk down the lane towards the marsh, leaving the Moore's Arms on your left. After 250 yards turn left up the narrow Hall Lane.

Turn off this lane on a signposted footpath and walk diagonally left across the field, aiming to the left of the farm buildings, to find a waymark and an earth bridge. Continue straight forward towards the trees where there is a ditchboard with a handrail and a public footpath signpost.

Cross Streetway to another wooden bridge over a wide drain and continue straight forward to yet another bridge and stile. Keeping the moat on your right, go through a fieldgate and then cross a stile leading to the lane and Wyberton village.

❷ Turn left at the white handgate into the churchyard just before reaching the lane. The church has a most unusual dedication to St Leodegar, Bishop of Autun in the 7th century. Do have a look at the outstanding gravestone to a Brigadier General at the entry to the path leading to the Hall. Turn left out of the churchyard down Church Lane. On reaching the road junction turn left along Low Road with the telephone box on your left.

❸ Continue straight forward at the crossroads for 300 yards to bear left onto Hall Lane at the Y-fork by Frampton village sign. Follow this quiet lane back to your starting point.

PLACES of INTEREST

There is much to see in nearby Boston. The splendid parish church of St Botolph was built in the early 14th century, its foundations being made 'secure' by large quantities of raw wood being added to the stone. Its famous tower is affectionately known as the **Boston Stump**. Visitors on Wednesdays and Saturdays can (if fit enough) climb the steep spiral staircase to enjoy the magnificent view that makes the effort worthwhile. Marked on the west front are dated flood marks, one being as recent as 21st January 1963, when a fish swam down the aisle. The **Guildhall Museum** in South Street was built in 1450 for the Guild of St Mary. It is best known for being the place where the Pilgrim Fathers were imprisoned in 1607 and put on trial. Open daily from 10 am to 5 pm (1.30 pm to 5 pm on Sundays). Telephone: 01205 365954. The **Maud Foster Windmill** in Willoughby Road was built in 1819 and is the tallest working windmill in England, having seven floors. It was restored in 1988 and works daily when the wind blows, producing stone-ground organic flour. Open Wednesday, and Friday and Saturday in August only, 10 am to 5 pm, and Sunday and Bank Holidays 2 pm to 5 pm. Telephone: 01205 352188. Three walk leaflets beginning at the Market Place are available at the Tourist Information Centre in Spain Lane. Telephone: 01205 356656.

WALK 16

BUTTERWICK

Length : 5 miles

Getting there: Butterwick village is 3/4 mile south of the A52 Boston–Skegness road, 4 miles east of Boston. Turn off the main road for Butterwick at a crossroads 1 mile east of the Hobhole Drain bridge.

Parking: Either in the Five Bells car park or in the church hall car park directly opposite.

Map: OS Landranger 131 Boston and Spalding area (GR 388450).

Butterwick, bypassed by the main road today, is a quiet marshland village between Boston and the sea. The local place name endings of -ton, -toft and -wick indicate Anglo-Saxon origins with strong Danish connections. In the Domesday Book there is ample evidence of a flourishing economy supporting a large population with more than the usual number of 'sokemen' or freemen, and two churches were recorded; one would be Butterwick and the other Freiston church, to the south-east.

St Andrew's at Butterwick is an old building of brick and stone, much restored in 1800. There is a large sycamore tree in the churchyard believed to have been

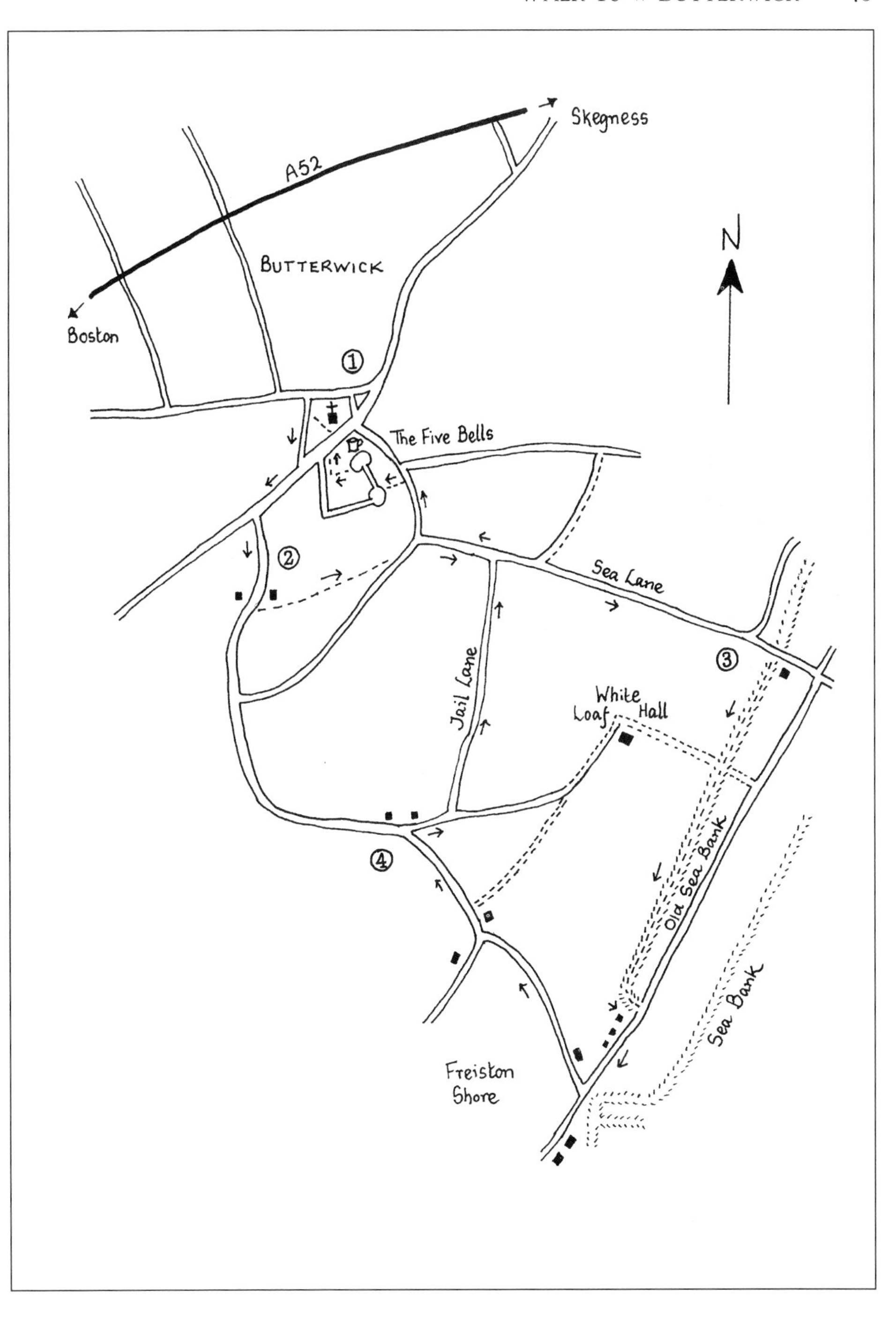
Skegness
A52
BUTTERWICK
Boston
N
①
The Five Bells
②
Sea Lane
③
Jail Lane
White
Loaf
Hall
④
Old Sea Bank
Sea Bank
Freiston
Shore

The village pub.

planted more than 300 years ago. On the little green in the village centre outside the Five Bells one of the four fingers of the directional signpost is labelled 'Seas end', pointing the way you will go for some of the walk. A very early school, Pinchbeck's, was dated 1659 and enlarged in 1878. It has now been replaced by a more modern building.

The name Freiston came from a colony of Frielanders who settled hereabouts, where today a village has grown up between the Hobhole Drain and the sea, which once came much further inland. Freiston and Butterwick are now 2 miles from the sea and it is still receding as new banks are built. The old mud flats are covered with a carpet of sand grasses and wildflowers only washed today by the highest tides.

The wildness of the marsh has been tamed by the construction of new sea banks, a practice that began with the Romans and continues to the present day, thanks to the labours of the inmates of North Sea Camp, an open prison.

The walk takes you by Freiston Shore, a strange place today for it was intended originally to be a seaside resort, the Skegness of this part of the Lincolnshire coast. At one time there used to be horse racing here on the reclaimed mud flats above the tidal marsh and two hotels, Plummers and the Marine, had large windows on the seaward side to enable people to watch the racing from the comfort of their chairs. The Marine is now a dangerous ruin and Plummers ceased trading a few years ago, although the mews have been made into attractive dwellings. The building of a railway to Skegness and its rapid development as a seaside resort ended Freiston Shore's dream.

This was once a smugglers' coast and there's many a tale of hobgoblins to discourage folk from wandering around out of doors after nightfall. White Loaf Hall, near the old sea bank, was said to be a smugglers' haunt. It has on one of its two stepped gables a stone shaped like a loaf and dated 1614. The first white loaf ever baked in England is said to have been made here, for until then brown bread had always been the staple diet. In 1711 John Linton became vicar of Butterwick and he resided at White Loaf Hall, from which a path led to the church. The third John Linton bought the redundant Freiston Priory in 1782 and he reclaimed much of the foreshore at that time. A story is told that when his orchard was repeatedly robbed he set up a man-trap as a deterrent and obtained a human leg from a friend who was a naval surgeon. His fruit was left unpicked from then onwards.

This remote and windswept corner of Lincolnshire is a different world from most of our other villages. Perhaps one could call it Cabbage Kingdom for this rich land recovered from the sea grows great numbers of vegetables destined for the London market in enormous lorries.

FOOD and DRINK

The Five Bells has a comfortable lounge and a separate dining room. Bar snacks and more substantial meals are served daily, both at lunchtime and in the evenings. Telephone: 01205 760282.

PLACES of INTEREST

The interesting little town of **Boston** is nearby. See Walk 15 for details of **Boston Stump**, the **Guildhall Museum** and the **Maud Foster Windmill**. South-east of Boston, at the end of the Hobhole Drain, is **Boston Haven**, the Pilgrim Fathers memorial and picnic place (GR 364402). North of Boston is the **Sibsey Trader Windmill**, open from April to August at various times. Telephone: 01604 730320.

THE WALK

❶ From the Five Bells car park cross the road to take the signposted footpath through the churchyard. Do not enter the paddock but turn right with the fence on your left through a handgate and onto Broughton Lane. Turn left down the lane to Church Road and the Old Brew House. Turn right along Church Street becoming School Lane. After 250 yards turn left up Girls School Lane and continue to the old school.

❷ Turn left on a signposted path at the old school to walk across the playground and to the left-hand corner of the playing field where there is an obvious gap in the hedge. Walk forward to cross the footbridge on the left and then continue forward to the lane where there is a footpath signpost. On reaching Sea Lane after turning left walk away from the village by turning right for about 3/4 mile and then right on the top of the sea bank on a signposted path with the drain on your immediate right. Chimnies (sic) and its garden is on the left.

❸ Continue along this bank for another 3/4 mile and then follow it round to the left until you meet the road. Turn right at the road past the old coastguard station and walk on for about 500 yards to have a look at all that remains of the abandoned holiday resort of Freiston Shore. Return and walk up Shore Road with White Loaf Hall over on the right. Continue past Cold Harbour to the T-junction.

❹ Turn right for only a few yards (signposted 'White Loaf Hall') and then left up Jail Lane. Continue on this lane until it joins Sea Road. Turn left on Sea Road and walk past Dove Lane. Ignoring the first two turnings on the left, take the new tarmac path alongside Hazlemere, 20 Sea Lane. Almost immediately on reaching the new estate road turn right up the cul de sac and then left at the top on another tarmac track into Prince William Drive. Turn right along the drive to Butterwick Road and right again to the car park.

WALK 17

WOOLSTHORPE BY COLSTERWORTH

Length : $6^1/_2$ miles

Getting there: From the Stamford–Grantham section of the A1 turn off the trunk road 7 miles south of Grantham onto the B6403, westwards to Colsterworth, just north of the railway bridge. If proceeding northwards on the A1 the turn is a mile beyond the Colsterworth roundabout.

Parking: Turn left almost immediately after leaving the A1 onto a section of the old road blocked at the village end to make a cul de sac. Park by the public footpath signpost.

Map: OS Landranger 130 Grantham and surrounding area (GR 931244).

Beware, for there are two Woolsthorpes in Lincolnshire, not many miles apart. The name comes from 'Ulestanestorp', meaning outlying farmstead or hamlet of a man named Wulstan, Wulf or Ulf.

At one time Colsterworth lay astride the Great North Road but it was bypassed when the highway was realigned and renamed the A1. The local council, anxious to preserve the separate identities of Colsterworth and Woolsthorpe, bars the building of new properties between the two

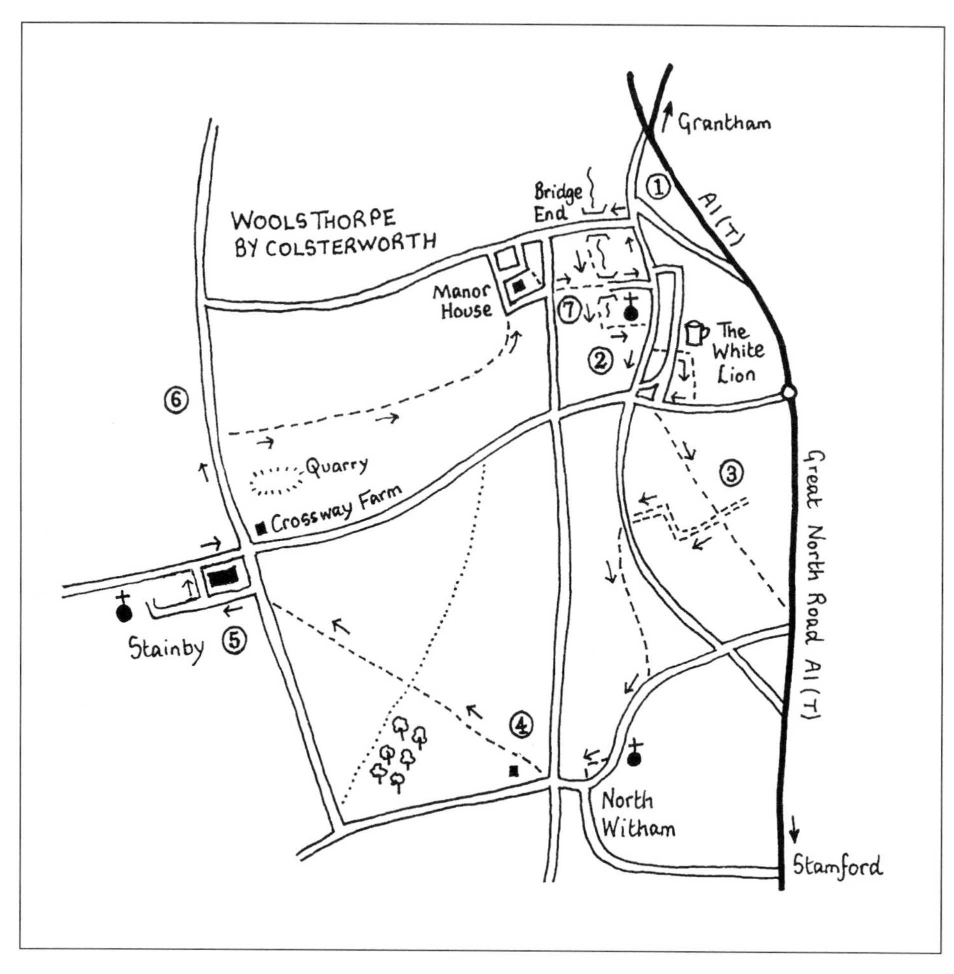

villages although some infilling has taken place. In 1086 the Domesday Book treated Woolsthorpe as part of Colsterworth, belonging to the Archbishop of York, Aeldred, who was a Saxon. Earl Edwin, the Queen's 'thaine' had a manor at Colsterworth recorded in Domesday.

The nucleus of Colsterworth village lies along the High Street where, in the heyday of the coaching trade, there were ten inns at one time, now reduced to only one, the White Lion. Most of the old coaching stops have been made into business premises or private dwellings.

The Saxons built a church here after the Romans left and the Normans pulled it down and rebuilt it. On New Year's Day in 1643 a child was brought here from Woolsthorpe and christened Isaac Newton and a page in the register still records that event. Today there is a Newton Memorial Chapel, rebuilt in the scientist's memory, that includes a sundial carved with a penknife when he was a boy of nine.

The flooded former mineral working at Stainby.

In 1623 the manor house at Woolsthorpe was bought by Robert Newton, and it was here that his grandson was born.

People have been visiting Woolsthorpe to pay homage to the great man ever since his death in 1727; no doubt trying to experience for themselves the atmosphere which led him to formulate his momentous law of gravitation and to hear the story of the famous apple tree. The property now belongs to the National Trust. Some of the more notable names in the visitors book include Albert Einstein, Stephen Hawking and Patrick Moore.

The walk takes you by the manor house after visiting Stainby which must surely be one of the quietest places in the county.

THE WALK

❶ From the old A1 road, now bypassed, take the signposted footpath across the small field away from the busy A1 — the path goes both ways. On reaching the lane turn right along Bridge End and then left down Woolsthorpe Road. At the road bridge with the farm shop on your left, cross the bridge and go down the steps onto the signposted footpath with the infant river Witham on your left. After only a few yards climb the waymarked stile on your right and turn left along the field edge to a stile in the left-hand corner of the pasture field. Go through the double tunnel and on arriving at the track turn left up the lane to the road bridge. Just beyond the bridge turn right on a clear, signposted path that becomes a delightful hollow way uphill with the church on your left.

❷ Cross the lane and walk straight forward with the White Lion on your left. Turn right at the road and, after a few yards, turn left up Ropewalk with the Methodist church on your left. This track becomes a good tarmac path. Cross the estate road and proceed forward around the metal barrier. The tarmac track gives way to a pleasant green path. At the end turn right down Bourne Road for 250 yards, then go left on a signposted path through the wooden fieldgate next to the house numbered '16'. Turn left at the end of the fence and after a few yards go diagonally right across the field to the left-hand corner where there is a stile and a waymark. Walk downhill, aiming some 30 yards to the left of the hedge junction where you will find a post and a waymark. Continue uphill on the same line and at the top right-hand field corner there is a waymark post.

❸ Turn right on the good green track, walking in the direction of Stainby church spire almost 2 miles away. Cross directly over Stamford Road to follow the sign-posted path with a stile. Aim across the pasture field towards the trees to the left of North Witham church spire. There is a stile in the fence at the break in the hedge and 120 yards further on another stile and waymark. Now walk towards the road to a fieldgate at the roadside. Turn right down to the ford over the river Witham and into North Witham village. The church is well worth a visit. Leaving the church, turn right up the signposted footpath opposite the church gate. Continue forward on reaching Rectory Road with the Old Rectory on your right. Go straight across Old Post Lane to the village hall — a good place for an apple stop.

❹ Take the signposted footpath by the village hall. Cross the hall field and play area to a handgate and footpath signpost. Walk forward just to the right of the electricity post, aiming for the centre of Stainby Warren Wood, to a fence, stile and waymark post. Walk to the bottom of the dip in the field and on to the left-hand corner of the next small field by a hedge, crossing the remnants of a ruined rabbit warren wall en route. Here there is a ditchboard and waymark. Turn left for only

PLACES of INTEREST

Woolsthorpe Manor, birthplace of Sir Isaac Newton, is open from Easter to October, Wednesday to Sunday afternoons, plus Bank Holiday Mondays (closed Good Friday). Telephone: 01476 860338. **Geeson Bros Motor Cycle Museum and Workshop** in Water Lane, South Witham exhibits 83 British bikes dating back to 1913. Telephone: 01572 762280. East of south Witham is **Morkery Wood**, a Forestry Commission wood with picnic tables, woodland walks and a nature trail.

FOOD and DRINK

The White Lion, at Colsterworth, offers a wide range of sandwiches, basket meals, home-made pies, meals from the griddle and salads, in comfortable surroundings. There is a function room, restaurant, beer garden and patio area. Telephone: 01476 860381.

a few yards until you reach the hedge, then go diagonally right uphill with the wood across the field over on your left and the hedgeline way over on the right. Continue almost to the left-hand corner of the field and beyond the edge of the wood. Go through the wide gap in the hedge and immediately proceed diagonally right across the small area of rough ground to a fence, stile and footpath signpost. From here walk directly towards Stainby church. After the stile in the last field before the road change your line to almost the right-hand corner of the field. There is a stile in the fence, a waymark and a footpath signpost. Cross the green lane and then cross Gunby Road.

❺ Turn right briefly down Gunby Road, over the road bridge, and then proceed left down the delightful Water Lane into Stainby. Take the left-hand fork to keep the magnificent Springwater House on your right. Turn right at the next lane with a splendid view of the church across the field on your left. Turn right and then left along Middle Street and right on reaching the Buckminster Road to proceed down to the crossroads. Turn left here with Crossway Farm on your right. Walk along Skillington Road for almost 800 yards, passing the deep, abandoned quarry on the right.

❻ Turn off the road on a signposted path with the hedge on your immediate right. After 400 yards turn left through the obvious gap in the hedge and proceed to the right with the hedge now on your right until you reach the field corner. Go through the clear gap in the hedge and walk forward to the stile in the cross hedge, then follow the clearly defined route diagonally left to the bottom left-hand corner of the field. Cross the hedge on the left before reaching the old metal field gate and turn right down the field to the stile in the next cross hedge (waymark) by the corner. At Water Lane turn right for a few yards and then go left up the tarmac path. Turn right at the lane to see Woolsthorpe Manor and gardens. Access to the house is from the small car park in Water Lane. Leave the lane by Manor View Cottage and go right again on the signposted path. Go over the stile and cross the field diagonally to the left-hand corner where there is another stile, a signpost and a metal gate by the road junction.

❼ Cross the road to take the signposted path with a stile. Go up the embankment steps over an old mineral railway line and down the other side to a stile. Walk down the right-hand edge of the field with a small stream on your right. On reaching the path you used on the outward journey turn right through the double tunnel and when you reach the road walk left uphill to the church. Turn left at the top to walk down the village street and then go right on the signposted path you used earlier. This brings you to the old main road where your walk began.

WALK 18

CORBY GLEN

Length : $4^1/_2$ miles

Getting there: Turn eastwards off the A1 at Colsterworth roundabout onto the A151 Bourne road for $4^1/_2$ miles to Corby Glen. Alternatively, turn off the A52 Grantham-Boston road at Grantham roundabout onto the B1176 for 8 miles to Corby Glen, via Boothby Pagnell.

Parking: In Corby Glen square by the market cross.

Map: OS Landranger 130 Grantham and surrounding area (GR 000250).

Corby Glen is a good stone-built village, situated amidst delightful wooded countryside in a predominantly farming area. The name was formally adopted in 1955 to avoid confusion with the town of Corby in nearby Northamptonshire. In the market square is an 18th-century cross on a medieval base and it was here that 'May servants' were hired for the year. Corby got its market charter from King Henry III in 1239 and one of the witnesses to the document was Simon de Montfort, Earl of Leicester. There is no longer a weekly market but the village is still quite famous

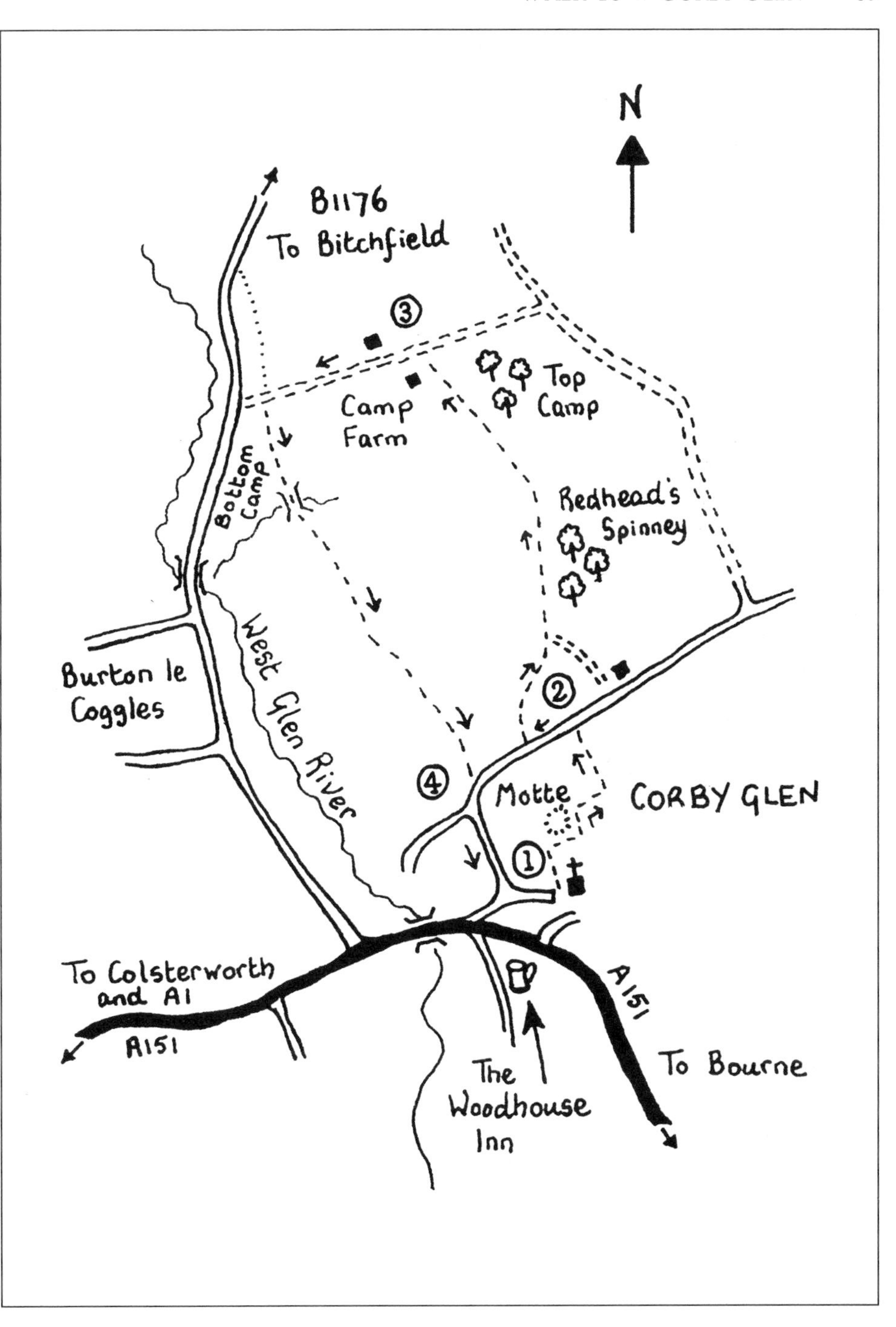
N
B1176
To Bitchfield
③
Top Camp
Camp Farm
Bottom Camp
Redhead's Spinney
Burton le Coggles
West Glen River
②
④
Motte
CORBY GLEN
①
To Colsterworth and A1
A151
A151
To Bourne
The Woodhouse Inn

The path near Camp Farm.

for its ancient sheep fair held in October each year. At one time up to 5,000 sheep were brought here to be auctioned — this is the end of the farming financial year and tenant farmers often had to sell their sheep in order to settle rent arrears. October 1988 saw the 750th anniversary of the fair and a week of celebrations took place. The fair is three days of fun with the Rutland Morris Men, skittles as a popular sideshow, a produce display, a photographic exhibition and handicrafts. In recent years there have not been many contestants for the traditional three-legged race around the remaining three pubs — in spite of free beer!

At one time there were nine hostelries in the town and one of them, The Fighting Cocks, was said to be haunted. One tenant only spent 27 days in the pub and on his last night he slept in his car! The original cock-pit is now blocked off in the cellar.

During redecoration of St John's church in 1939 discovery was made of a remarkable series of wall paintings said to be the finest in Lincolnshire. In medieval times few people could read or write and it was common practice to illustrate stories from the bible by painting on church walls. As progress was made from one story to the next the pictures could be covered in whitewash and further paintings added. Corby must have provided a pleasant living for there were only five vicars in 220 years, which surely must be something of a record. The quaint epitaph for John Wright, a 19th-century auctioneer, situated just off the path outside the church is well worth seeking.

One of Corby Glen's historic buildings is the picturesque Grammar School, founded under the will of Charles Read in 1669. For 240 years the school educated the area's more prosperous sons until it was closed in 1909. It is now the Willoughby Library, Art Gallery and Reading Room through a trust founded in November 1965 by the Earl of Ancaster and dedicated to the memory of his son, Lord Timothy Willoughby. One of the villagers who attended the opening ceremony was someone who left the school in 1898. Although he had lived in Corby all his life he had not set foot in the school since the day he left and he thought it smaller inside than he remembered it.

Corby Glen is unusual in having a substantial Roman Catholic chapel. It was built originally by Lord Clifford for his house at Irnham where there was a long history of links with Catholicism. During the difficult times of the late 1500s Catholics faced fines and imprisonment, and there was at least one priest's hole at Irnham Hall. At one time a crucifix held by Mary Queen of Scots at her execution was kept there. When Irnham Hall was sold the chapel became a centre of a legal dispute which was resolved by moving it to Corby around 1855.

The walk is a most interesting and attractive one in pleasant, undulating countryside where it is not unlikely that you may see deer.

FOOD and DRINK

The Woodhouse Inn, the only pub that serves food at present, is on the main road above the village. It started life as the New Inn and was later renamed after the new owners of the Irnham Estate. Today the old stabling has been converted to accommodate three en-suite bedrooms. There is a pleasant garden and an unusual outdoor oven. Bar or restaurant meals are served, as well as some fine ales and good whiskies. Telephone: 01476 550316.

PLACES of INTEREST

Grimsthorpe Castle, off the A51 to the east of Corby Glen, is Lincolnshire's best kept secret. There is a 3,000 acre Capability Brown landscaped park with lakes and ancient woods, nature trails, the Coach House Tea Room, a red deer herd, a woodland adventure playground, a family cycle trail, formal and woodland gardens and an unusual ornamental vegetable garden. The park and gardens are open from 11 am until 6 pm and the castle from 2 pm. For more information telephone: 01778 591205. **Boothby Pagnell Norman Manor House**, to the north of Corby, is open any day by appointment. Telephone: 01476 585374.

THE WALK

❶ From the Market Place walk up to the church to examine the wall paintings and to seek the quaint epitaph. Retrace your steps from the church to turn right up a signposted public footpath before you reach the square. Follow this clear path around the field edges to the road, diverting halfway along to look at the remains of the castle motte on your left about 200 yards north-west of the church.

❷ Upon reaching the lane turn left

downhill for 170 yards and then right up a signposted footpath over a stile, only a few yards before the Corby Glen sign. Walk up the short hollow way to another stile and then head forward towards the electricity pylon. Continue on this same line to the left-hand field corner. Cross the farm track and head forward, aiming for the left-hand edge of Redhead's Spinney. From there walk towards the clear gap in the hedge and a wooden electricity post and then straight forward to the next hedge with a footbridge and waymark. Continue forward on the same line, parallel to the wood over on the right. At the next hedge gap there are two waymarks for two public paths. Ignore the one on the right and continue forward to the farm track with Camp Farm on your left. This is a public right of way known as a BOAT (a byway open to all traffic).

❸ Turn left down this byway past Camp Farm and 200 yards beyond the farm turn left across the field on a clear, signposted footpath. Proceed down into the hollow, over the footbridge and up the slope on the other side. Aim to the right of the electricity pylon towards an obvious hedge gap with a waymark. In the next field cross to the field corner on the right where there is a stile in the wooden fencing. Go over the long paddock with a dip to the top right-hand corner of the field where there is another waymark by the wooden fieldgate. Walk forward about 150 yards with a wooden fence on your left to the next fieldgate. Go through the allotments with a green house on your right to a metal fieldgate. Pass through into the Wheatsheaf Yard; this is one of the redundant public houses.

❹ Turn briefly right and then proceed up the village street with Our Lady of Mount Carmel Roman Catholic church on your left and the ancient Fighting Cocks on the right. The market square is at the top of the street.

WALK 19

SURFLEET AND SURFLEET SEAS END

Length : $2^1/_2$ miles

Getting there: Turn off the A16 (T) between Spalding and Boston, by Surfleet church with its leaning spire, to continue for 2 miles along a secondary road to Surfleet Seas End. If you are driving northwards on the A16, Surfleet church is about 4 miles beyond Spalding and you turn right on the secondary road after crossing the river Glen road bridge.

Parking: The landlord has given permission for walkers' cars to be left in the car park of the Ship Inn.

Map: OS Landranger 131 Boston and Spalding area (GR 281295).

Surfleet — its name literally means 'sour stream' — is a fenland village dominated by poplars silhouetted against the flat, open landscape. In the centre of the village a sign 'Surfleet Seas End — 2 miles' from where this walk begins pinpoints the one-time nearness of the sea. Indeed, as late as 1738, the river Glen was a tidal stream emptying itself directly into the Wash. Domesday mentioned two salt pans in Surfleet ('fleet' indicates a tidal creek). These salt pans, whereby marine salt was

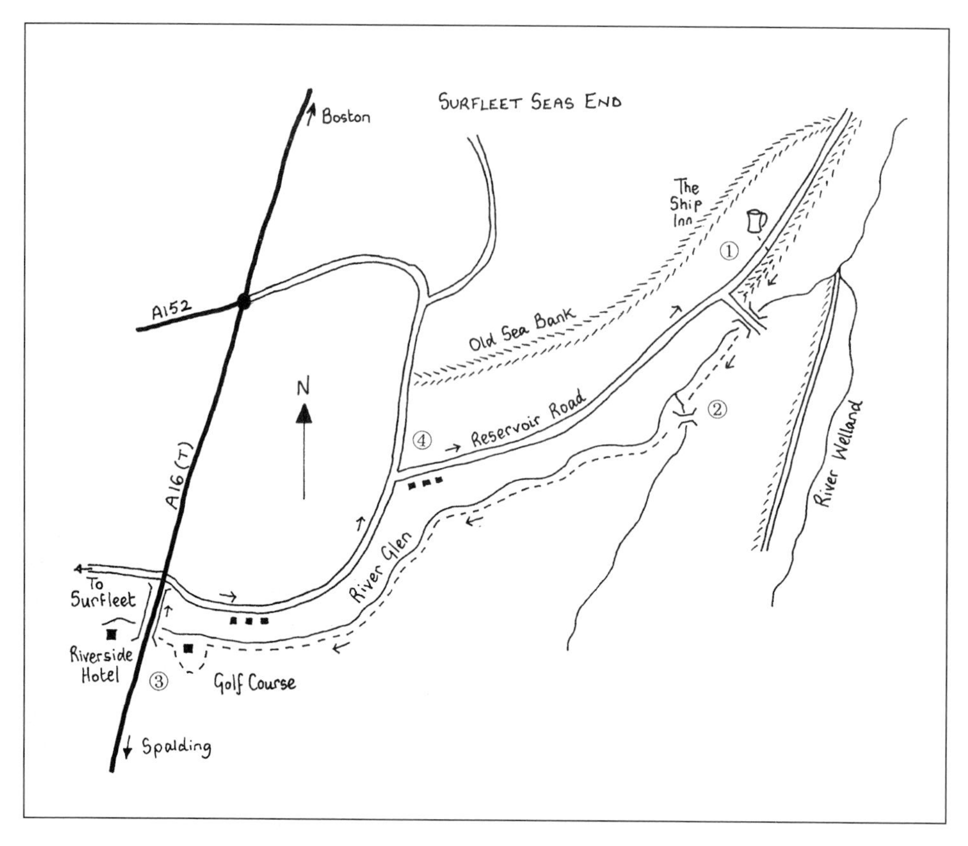

obtained by evaporation, were much prized and a real source of income to people dwelling on the coastal margins of the fen. It was an ancient craft and many old roads were saltways where this valuable commodity was transported by packhorses or carts to inland towns and cities.

The river Glen, once known as the Bourne Ee, meanders some 30 miles from Boothby Pagnell to join the river Welland on the seaward side of the Surfleet Sluice outfall. Both rivers were once important means of communication, the Glen affording an excellent waterway between the Welland and the Roman Car Dyke.

For centuries Surfleet's inhabitants were engaged in avoiding constantly threatening floods for the sea banks established by the Romans had, on their departure, been allowed to fall into disrepair. During the Middle Ages the whole economy of Fenland relied on the good condition of its sewers and drains. As early as 1362 the Riding Jurors reported that Surfleet sea banks were too low and after a great storm in 1810 the sheep were swimming in the pastures. The deepening of the river Glen formed part of Sir Thomas Lovell's fenland reclamation scheme, for silting had proved a great hazard in all the local waterways. In the early part of the 17th

Boats moored on the river Glen.

century the Welland was found to be so choked for want of dyking that travellers were forced to carry their boats by cart for 3 or 4 miles. A few years later it was said that there wasn't enough water in the Welland to drown a mouse.

Today the river Glen is a real asset, with boating and fishermen along Surfleet's summer retreat, known once as 'the grand Bason' when a sluice was built there in 1739. 'The Reservoir', as it is now known, has a colony of weekend homes on the peaceful river bank, passed on the walk. Only a few steps away on the seaward side of the sluice yachts are at anchor awaiting an incoming tide to take them 'below' to the Deeps.

Gosberton Church is very high
Surfleet Church is all awry.

This is an old rhyme for the 600 year old tower leans westwards at an angle so perilous that the tip of the spire is 6 feet out of the perpendicular. The explanation is that the boggy marshland results in subsidence. It was said scurrilously by locals that the tower was really bowing to an honest lawyer — once wrongly deemed a rarity. The musket shot holes on the outside of the north door are said to have been made by Cromwellian soldiery and the south window is a medley of painted glass dug up from the churchyard after their billeting in the church.

Flax, once a local crop, was usually sown in May and pulled up at 'old Lammas' (August), bound in sheaves, soaked in water, laid out in a dish for two or three weeks, broken, swingled and sent to market. However, industrial pollution was a problem even in the late 19th century for the authorities ordered that neither flax nor hemp should be watered in the sewers on pain of forfeiture.

The Ship Inn was probably built around 1642 at the time when Scottish and Irish prisoners of war and Dutch labourers were working on the drainage of the fens. Fenmen hated the idea of the fens being drained and boycotted working on any drainage schemes, therefore other labour had to be imported.

Daphne Ledward, green-fingered gardening broadcaster, lives in the picturesque cottage, Little Thatch, whose flower beds are much admired by villagers and can be seen on your walk along Seas End Road.

After stopping off to admire the church in Surfleet, enjoy a relaxing stroll along the bank of the Glen river. Watch the small boats at anchor in the tidal reach below the sluice, awaiting high tide before proceeding down to the Wash. Then take in the quiet village street with some attractive gardens and finally on to a most pleasant hostelry, renowned for good food, and the walker-friendly host at the Ship.

The Macmillan Way is a 235 mile Long Distance Footpath from Oakham, Rutland to Abbotsbury in Dorset. In late 1997, an extension was created from Oakham to Boston, Lincolnshire making a new Coast to Coast Path. This extension route now goes through Surfleet Seas End and along the river Glen part of your walk.

PLACES of INTEREST

There is much to see and do in and around Spalding. The **Ayscoughfee Hall Museum** in Churchgate is open all year and includes galleries on the landscape, history and people of the fens. Telephone: 01775 725468. **Springfields Gardens** in Camelgate covers 30 acres and includes a tropical palm house, bulb museum, carp lake and restaurant. Telephone: 01775 724843. There is also a bulb museum at the **Birchgrove Garden Centre** in Surfleet Road, open March to October. Telephone: 01775 680490. Then there is the **Pinchbeck Engine and Land Drainage Museum**, off West Marsh Road, exhibiting a steam beam engine driving a scoop wheel erected in 1833. Open from Easter to October 10 am to 4 pm. Telephone: 01775 725468.

FOOD and DRINK

The Ship Inn is a most pleasant country inn with two letting bedrooms, a freehouse serving a range of hand-pulled real ale, mainly Marston's, where you will find a warm and homely welcome with excellent bar and restaurant meals. Its traditional link with the sea is demonstrated by a notice in the lounge stating 'A ship has been sighted in this quarter engaged in the unlawful act of smuggling', dated 19 October, 1782. These days a launch can be booked for sailing upriver and there is free fishing on the Glen for guests. Telephone: 01775 680384.

THE WALK

❶ From the Ship Inn car park climb the sea bank to turn right along the top of the pleasant grassy embankment. You will discover that there is a fascinating hidden assembly of boats lying at different angles depending upon the state of the tide. Upon reaching the lane turn left for 50 yards, go over the bridge and then turn right down the steps onto a signposted footpath with the river Glen now on your right and a collection of varied weekend dwellings on the left.

❷ At the stile on the left of the wooden barrier, climb the slope and continue forward for 50 yards to where the concrete track turns left. Turn right over the small bridge (waymark) above the subsidiary lock gates and continue walking forward with the river on your immediate right and the golf course on the left. Note the golf warning: 'If a shout of "Fore" is heard take evasive action.' There are some lovely trees here and fascinating views of the attractive gardens behind the houses across the river. Upon reaching the golf course bungalow continue straight forward to the obvious handgate, stile and footpath signpost.

❸ Turn right by the steps and follow the tarmac track under the roadway *only* if you wish to adjourn to the Riverside Hotel. Otherwise turn right on the roadbridge and right again almost immediately up Seas End Road, passing Little Thatch on the right.

❹ After 700 yards turn right up Reservoir Road and continue through the hamlet until you reach the Ship Inn.

WALK 20

GEDNEY HILL

Length : $1^3/_4$ or $4^1/_2$ miles

Getting there: Turn eastwards off the A1073 Crowland–Spalding road $1^1/_2$ miles north of Crowland onto the B1166 leading first to Holbeach Drove and then to Gedney Hill. Alternatively, turn off the A17 (T) road at Long Sutton roundabout onto the B1390 to Sutton St James, then follow minor roads to Sutton St Edmund and on to Gedney Hill, some 11 miles from Long Sutton.

Parking: There is a car park at the T-junction directly opposite the Cross Keys inn on Hillgate, Gedney Hill.

Map: OS Landranger 142 Peterborough (GR 339114).

This silt land is a strange, remote world, quite different from any other part of the county, offering a unique experience that well repays the considerable effort of actually getting there.

There are half a dozen Gedneys and some 15 miles between Gedney Drove End on the coast to Gedney Hill, just over a mile from Lordship End on the Cambridgeshire side of the county boundary. Gedney Hill is a straggling village, boasting three pubs even today, with long, straight roads leading to it across the Bedford Level.

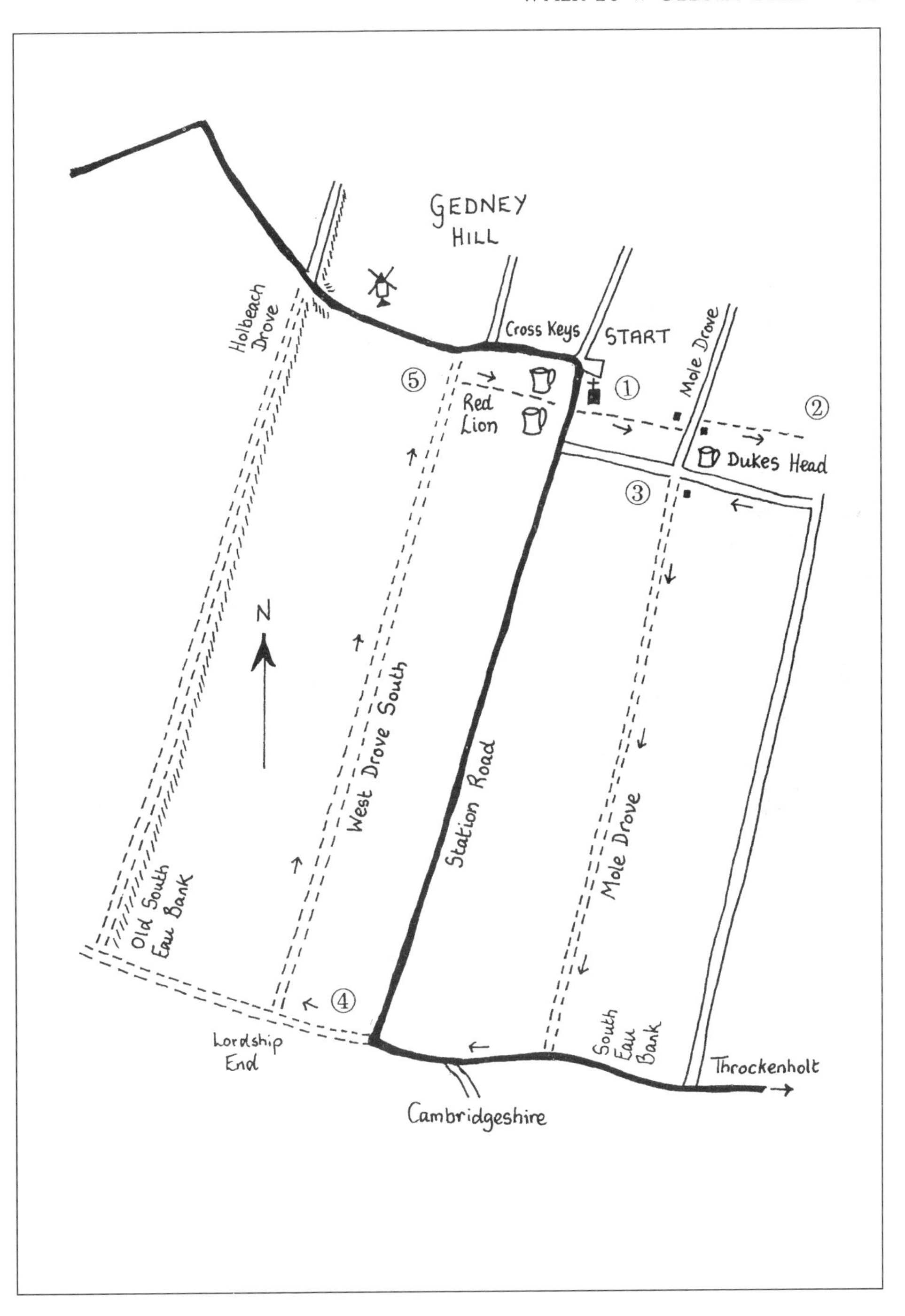
GEDNEY HILL
Holbeach Drove
Cross Keys
START
Mole Drove
⑤
①
②
Red Lion
Dukes Head
③
N
West Drove South
Station Road
Mole Drove
Old South Eau Bank
④
Lordship End
South Eau Bank
Throckenholt
Cambridgeshire

One of the three pubs to be found in Gedney Hill.

The Rev Richard Lawson Gates, one-time vicar of Gedney, was thinking about these broad, flat lands and the great dome of the Fen sky when he wrote:

Green, rose and gold
Heaven to behold . . .
With a great bronze glow
Day dies slow.

It is now over 200 years since this part of Lincolnshire was drained by Dutch engineers and it still lies below the high tide level of the Wash. The area is likened to Holland for there are few walls or hedges and the man-made roads are invariably straight and narrow. A spot height of three metres at the far end of the village demonstrates how such a word as 'hill' can be interpreted in this part of Lincolnshire.

Gedney Hill came into being sometime after the making of the Common Dyke in 1241, and the new South Eau Drain was cut in 1631. Flooding, not only from the sea but also fresh water from the land, was always a problem. The original name, Gedenai, was taken from the enclosure of spikes which in Anglo-Saxon times was used to protect the 'island' from roving bands of sea-raiders coming into the Wash from the mainland of Europe. The sea, in those days, was much further inland.

The drainage of the Lincolnshire Fens

has a long history. The Romans played a part although much of their work was later obliterated. In the Middle Ages sea walls were built, driving back the sea or holding back its encroachments. Successive inundations and the silting up of the channels undid much of the work. From 1600 onwards Vermuyden and his helpers were called in to provide expertise. He abandoned the older practice of trying to keep the river channels clear and cut new channels shorter than the old ones. The theory was to make water flow faster and prevent the rivers silting up. The channels, however, needed constant attention to keep them open and, as time went on, the land sank as a result of drainage making the peat shrink. Eventually the inner fen was lower than the outer fen, lower in fact than the river that drained them, so windmills became necessary to raise the water in the channels to push it off the land. Many windmills were needed and, at one time, 63 stood alongside the banks of the Forty Foot Drain. But they did not stop the flooding and it was the development of the steam pump, which did not rely upon a fickle wind, that eventually proved effective. Throughout the whole of this period there was bitter opposition from locals whose way of life was dramatically changed by the drainage of the fens.

FOOD and DRINK

The three pubs in Gedney Hill are the Dukes Head in Highstock Lane (telephone: 01406 330275), the Red Lion in Hillgate (telephone: 01406 330539) and the Cross Keys, also in Hillgate (telephone: 01406 330569).

PLACES of INTEREST

The **Butterfly and Falconry Park** at Long Sutton is open daily. It is one of Britain's largest indoor butterfly gardens, with hundreds of exotic species flying free. The Falconry Centre houses owls, hawks and falcons. Check for the time of flying displays. Telephone: 01406 363833. At Terrington St Clement, off the A17 west of King's Lynn, the **African Violet Centre** is open daily, with 4,000 blooms and a wide variety of types and colours. Telephone: 01553 828374.

In 1982 Gedney was visited by over 400 people whose surname was Gedney, Gadney or Gidney. They travelled from Canada, America, Australia and all over Britain to take part in a special church service. On this special occasion the postmaster was given authority for letters and postcards to be franked 'Gedney'.

Enjoy a leisurely stroll taking in some of the remoteness of the Fen dominated by wide horizons and the straight lines of footpaths, drainage channels and drove roads across reclaimed land. Away from the main road, curiously called Hillgate in the village, it is unlikely that you will meet anyone en route off the metalled highway. Yet the area is intensely farmed and there is evidence all around of farming activities on some of the most productive agricultural land in Britain. The walk provides an easy and fascinating introduction to an area of very different countryside than that found in much of the rest of the county.

THE WALK

❶ From the car park turn left down Hillgate towards the church. Turn left off the road on the signposted public footpath through the churchyard and proceed straight forward on a clear path over the substantial bridge and onto the road known as Mole Drove. Turn left along Mole Drove for 60 yards and then follow the signposted path on the right leading you straight forward to the footpath signpost on Lutton Gate Road.

❷ Turn right down Lutton Gate Road for 200 yards and then right again at the junction, along to the Dukes Head. At this point, if you have opted for the shorter walk, it is possible to walk forward along Highgate as far as the Red Lion and there to turn right along Hillgate back to your starting point.

❸ For the longer walk, turn left opposite the Dukes Head down the unsurfaced green lane that is a continuation of Mole Drove. After almost exactly 1 mile climb the bank to go through the field gate to the winding lane following the top of the Old South Eau Bank. Turn right along this road for 700 yards.

❹ Where the road turns sharp right to Gedney Hill village continue forward along the surfaced track on top of the old sea bank. There is a warning about it being unsuitable for motors. After 500 yards on top of the bank turn right down West Drove South, which becomes a tarmac lane.

❺ Almost at the end of this surfaced lane turn right on a clear signposted footpath towards the church. Turn left down Hillgate back to your starting point opposite the Cross Keys.